Spirit of Champions

Great Achievers Reveal How to Unify Body, Mind and Spirit

Spirit of Champions

Great Achievers Reveal
How to Unify Body, Mind and Spirit

Lyle Nelson
and
Thorn Bacon

BookPartners, Inc.
Wilsonville, Oregon

BookPartners, Inc.
P.O. Box 922
Wilsonville, Oregon 97070

In 1991, the Mount Hood Nordic Ski Foundation united a small band of athletes in Oregon who believed that achieving excellence required a high commitment from the body, mind and spirit. These athletes have won too many national championships to record, fourteen Olympic berths collectively (we honestly don't count them up), and even one world championship. Their bond to support each other is unbreakable and wonderful. This book represents the ideals they stand up for, and in many cases, pioneered. With true love, and thanks for the lessons, to: Bill, Lara, Ben, Julie, Justin, Maggie, Sam, Joan. And Angie — who is now looking over all of us.

Acknowledgements

To expose, via the permanence of print, your most precious, most personal, and most introspective thoughts about the spiritual nature of being human requires extraordinary courage and consciousness. We acknowledge those individuals profiled in this book who, acting out of passion to help others along the sacred journey called life, shared themselves so others may learn who they are.

Table of Contents

Foreword

*The winds of grace are blowing perpetu-
ally, we only need raise our sails.*
– Sri Ramakrishna

By all accounts, this is an exciting time to be alive.
Never before has the human species become so connected
— politically, economically, and environmentally.
Excitement, however, can be perceived as either appealing
or frenetic. Typically, there is excitement with any kind of
change. And change, for better or worse, is in the air. While
some predict chaos with these winds of change, I intuitively
sense the opportunity for spiritual growth and the evolution
of human consciousness. Naturally, the winds of change
bring with them growing pains, but my hunch is that these
pains are indeed a sign of the spiritual growth of humanity.

The words spirit and wind (or breath) are often used
interchangeably in several cultures around the globe. So it
is no coincidence that the expression the "winds of

— 1 —

change" carries with it the inference of divine grace on the human journey. In other words, the winds of change usher in the winds of grace. We access this grace, this inspiration when we have the courage to raise our sails and explore new horizons rather than hide in fear. As the expression goes, "A ship is safe in port, but that's not what ships were built for."

The metaphor of the champion athlete serves as one of the best ways to articulate the essence of human spirituality. To exercise our inner resources (e.g., humor, optimism, courage, faith, humbleness, curiosity, creativity and compassion, what I call the muscles of the human soul), is to engage in the health of the human spirit. To deny the use of these inner resources is to see the muscles of the soul wither and atrophy. While there are some who say that we as a people, specifically the American culture, are in a period of spiritual bankruptcy, I prefer to use the expression spiritual dormancy. The spiritual essence within each one of us is never really absent, it merely lays dormant waiting to be called upon. I believe poet Maya Angelou said it best in her book, *Wouldn't Take Nothing For My Journey Now,* when she wrote these words:

> *I believe that Spirit is one and everywhere present. That it never leaves me. That in my ignorance, I may withdraw from it, but I can realize its presence the instant I return to my senses.... It is this belief in a power larger than myself and other than myself which allows me to venture into the unknown and even the unknowable. I cannot separate what I conceive as Spirit from my concept of God. Thus I believe that God is Spirit.*

During times of change, we are gently reminded of the divine essence which resides in each and every one of us. As science explores the farthest reaches of the universe, as researchers study the subtle intricacies of the mind-body-spirit connection, as ecologists grasp the full appreciation of our dynamic biosphere, the understanding becomes abundantly clear; the divine essence of life is everywhere present. Yet what is now coming to be realized by a core of remarkable scientists and intellectuals on the vanguard of human consciousness has been known for ages by the wisdom keepers, shamans, healers and sages of all cultures. This ancient (more accurately stated as ageless) wisdom never denied the recognition of our divine essence: it fully embraced it. This ageless wisdom is accessible to us at an intuitive level. The heroes and champions of all cultures draw upon this spirit with each breath and with each heartbeat. And we, like them, are no different.

The spirit of champions is nothing less than that which weaves the fabric of the human soul. As a birthright, not a gift, it manifests through the use of humor, compassion, faith, willpower, courage, optimism, humbleness, intuition and love. I have met countless champions in my travels on the human path. Some have been athletes; however, most fall in the category of what I call everyday heroes; ordinary people engaged in extraordinary endeavors that allow the human spirit to glow brightly. In doing so, they lead the way for others who follow closely in their footsteps. I am reminded of a man named Andrew, who at the age of thirteen had his life changed forever through a diving accident leaving him a quadriplegic. Today Andrew's strongest anatomical features are his funny bone and his smile, for it is humor which has helped him learn to cope with his situation. Andrew is now studying medicine where upon graduation he plans to be the ambassador for humor therapy in health care. Unbeknownst to him, he has already healed countless people by the smile and twinkle in his eye which in a subtle way says, "I know, I've been there. You can do it too."

Marie is another everyday hero. An alcoholic by the age of nineteen she faked her way through college, barely graduating with passing grades. A failed marriage and the loss of a job leaving her destitute at the age of twenty-four forced Marie to seriously contemplate suicide. It was faith in the form of prayer and grace through the gentle hand of synchronicity that brought her to a rehab program one afternoon and guided her on her path to recovery. She is now the mother of two teenage boys and has a successful career as bookstore owner on the West Coast providing inspiration for all who walk in her doors.

Heroes and champions are often found in the health care setting, particularly physicians and nurses who work in the emergency units of hospitals where life and death often hang in the balance for the patients admitted. As an ER nurse, Carolyn is one such champion. Strong-willed with a heart filled with compassion, Carolyn was known as "The Rock" of the emergency room. Yet even her foundations were shaken when late one night her husband walked onto the ER teary-eyed with a bundle of blankets in his arms; their six-month-old child dead of SIDS (sudden infant death syndrome). The devastation lasted several months, yet soon the grief began the transformation into compassion, as Carolyn directed her energies to form a support group for parents of children who died of SIDS.

The energy of the mythic hero and the inspiration of the champion athlete archetype are neither cute metaphors nor images of false hope. They are reminders to each and every one of us of our highest human potential. Today, in these turbulent times of change, each and every one of us is called upon to be a champion, a hero and a mentor. Not a day goes by when we are not called upon to use the creative energy of spirit to rise to every occasion that challenges us to achieve our highest human potential, be it on the playing field, the office, home or highway. Within each one of us resides the makings of a hero, with each breath we inspire the spirit of champions. And as we raise our arms in victory, we touch the face of god.

Brian Luke Seaward, Ph. D.
Boulder, Colorado
Author of *Stand Like Mountain, Flow Like Water*

1

The Trial of Cross-Country Skier Tuck Miller

Why, in a book designed to reveal the "Champion's Way" — to achieve a more successful and rewarding life — have we devoted the next 20 pages to a story about a harrowing accident and heroic rescue? To celebrate the resilience of human life? To entertain? To showcase the remarkable physical ability of Tuck Miller and mental courage of Kim Jude? No!

As you will see, what Tuck Miller accomplished, as remarkable as it was, is not beyond what you are capable of when you align your physical, mental and spiritual energies. Deep down you must acknowledge that you have felt rare moments in your life, moments of great inspiration, moments of peace filled with a sense of immense power, and moments that lifted your life and lighted your imagination.

Most people experience such rare moments of inspiration, and on inspection realize they are reflec-

tions of the true self — a self capable of shining out with a thoughtful, light that is dazzling.

What do these fleeting moments say to us?

They tell us that we are much greater than we imagine, and if we believe in our potential, our confidence will be demonstrated in accomplishments whose stature may astonish us.

This concept is one reason we have told the Tuck Miller story. The second reason is to convince you that the challenges you will meet and surpass in life are no less and no more than you are prepared to meet. Your challenges may not be like those of Tuck Miller's, the cliff you climb may not be a snow-covered mountainside, but it could be just as daunting. Jonas Salk climbed his mountain, as did Joan of Arc and Martin Luther King. All of us are tested in life; if we prepare mentally, physically and spiritually, we will contribute to humankind that which is needed from us. It was Ralph Waldo Emerson who told us that "Life is a succession of lessons which must be lived to be understood."

Our third reason for telling Tuck's story is to ask the question: Where does spiritual energy come from? Tuck sensed that he was calling upon an energy source that hitherto had been unknown to him. Was it spiritual energy which had always resided in him that required a cause of great magnitude to reveal itself? Is it human to be imbued with an internal reserve that comes to the surface during those moments of overwhelming need? Or, as many religious and spiritual leaders suggest, is there an external source of energy, the Good Will of the universe, that can flow into us when we act to further this Good Will?

The answer to this question is always subjective. Is there something extra about us? It is a question as old as our yearning to gather the wisdom from the stars and place that wisdom into our hearts. It is the principal question about which this book is concerned. Throughout the text we will present objective information about "the something extra" that exists inside all of us. This will help you determine for yourself mankind's greatest source of energy. We will share with you anecdotes and stories of men and women who have tapped into "the something extra" to make their lives outstanding.

When Tuck Miller spotted the coyote in the middle of the icy road, it was drifting toward the truck in the dark like a blind, gray wraith, obscured then revealed in the headlamps by the shifting wind. Sheets of whirling snow, descending and rising in the swath of the truck's lights, like a curtain parting and closing, gave Tuck tantalizing glimpses of the creature, and he slammed on the brakes to avoid hitting the animal.

"Did you see him?" he asked Kim Jude, who was straining her eyes to see through the cleared path on the frozen windshield.

"Sort of. Oh, look, Tuck! There he is."

Tuck saw the animal once more, framed for an instant in the glare of the lights. Motionless, the wind raising the gray fur around his head and shoulders into a thick halo, the creature seem unconcerned that he had escaped being struck. He appeared to be waiting, staring straight ahead, oblivious of the storm, as if his gaze were searching for Tuck's eyes only. As suddenly as he had come out of the cloud of snow, the coyote faded as the wind shifted again, hiding him behind a wall of white, made dazzlingly bright by the reflection of the headlights.

The truck had skidded when Tuck had hit the brakes, and even though the four-wheel drive was engaged, driving conditions on the icy road were tricky.

"Boy, I'd better slow down," Tuck said to himself.

He thought about the coyote for a moment.

As a biathlete, a hiker in the summer, a cross-country skier in the winter who coursed through the hills and valleys and down the mountains of rugged Idaho, he had observed the habits of birds and animals in all the seasons. A coyote wandering in a snowstorm on a remote logging road in the mountains didn't make much sense.

Tuck felt uneasy, and he wasn't easily disturbed, yet, call it hunch or intuition, he had a strong conviction that the coyote was a warning. The animal had not appeared to be sick, lost, confused or frightened by the truck, but momentarily, he had stood like a living signpost in the white, swirling dark. Tuck decided not to voice his feeling of foreboding to Kim. She was a marvelous woman, with a good head on her shoulders, but, not without reason, she was a little edgy about how the trip to Orofino was turning out.

Twenty-nine-year-old Tuck Miller and his girlfriend, Kim Jude, a twenty-seven-year-old college student at Boise State University, had left McCall, Idaho, heading for Orofino on the Clearwater River, about two o'clock on Christmas Day in 1988. It was close to 7:30 p.m. when he braked to avoid hitting the coyote. A trip on a bright dry day of four hours on the two-lane paved country road, the journey to Orofino in winter with ice and snow and bitter whirling winds through mountainous northern Idaho, could be treacherous for motorists.

Tuck had embarked on the drive to visit his brother, Ryan, a woods worker whom Tuck had not seen for more than a year. He missed Ryan, and the trip was his last chance to visit him before the World Championship trials in Lake Placid, New York. Tuck, a captain in the Idaho National Guard, the organization which was sponsoring his athletic career, had worked hard to get himself in top physical condition for the trials. A superb skier and excellent rifle shot, he expected to qualify for the biathlon team, a step toward participation in the 1992 Winter Olympics to be held in Albertville, France.

Where Tuck had gotten into trouble on the drive to Orofino was when he decided to take the shortcut at Grangeville, leaving the main road to save time. The first thirty miles had been okay, but when the pavement ended, as he knew it would, the road became a narrow dirt pathway, frequented by logging trucks and farmers in spring, summer and fall, but largely abandoned in winter. It was not maintained by highway crews and, as Tuck and Kim soon discovered, it was swept by dangerous winds and coated with a layer of ice and snow, reducing motoring speed to a crawl.

Tuck had pushed his dependable Chevy pickup to within striking distance of Orofino on the precipitous Gilbert Grade — a snakelike series of switchbacks that descended sharply into the isolated town by dropping more than 4,000 feet in about seven miles.

Placing the Chevy into a lower gear, Tuck resolved to exercise greater prudence and care for the balance of the trip to Orofino. He could not shake the idea that the coyote had been a warning, and he steered the pickup closer to the high bank on the right side of the road. Above him the mountain plateau, coated with a heavy layer of snow, rose a few hundred feet above the road. On his left side, just a few feet from where he was seated behind the wheel, the road dropped off. It was a 2,500-foot plunge down the steep mountainside from the road to the Clearwater River.

As Tuck carefully aimed his pickup down the icy road, he saw on his right about two hundred feet up from the highway a farmhouse with Christmas lights shining in the front window. It was a welcome sight as he drove on, and, oddly, he thought, it was good to know the location of the cheery farmhouse in case something happened.

"Quit borrowing trouble," he said to himself sternly.

He realized there was more openness on the left side of the truck now. There lay a yawning chasm and, for the first time since he started the trip, he began to feel anxious. The whiteout — a cloud of snow that could roll in as dense as fog in the mountains — was growing thicker by the minute, and he worried, as he cautiously applied the brakes, that if it got much worse he'd be driving in the blind. The idea was scary because, with the absence of a guardrail on the left of the road as a visible guide and buffer in case he swung too far in the wrong direction, he could drive over the edge.

It was Kim who put his own thoughts into words when she said, "Tuck I'm frightened. It's getting worse outside. Maybe we should stop."

Tuck had been debating that very decision himself, for the whiteout had thickened. The trouble was a whiteout could last for hours or dissipate in minutes. Now, the world outside the warm cab of the truck was almost like the inside of a cotton ball. He and Kim were surrounded by a smothering whiteness which the headlamps of the truck pierced only to the depth of a few feet. It was so thick that the right side of the mountain, the side Tuck had been hugging, was entirely obscured.

Already, Tuck had reduced his forward momentum to less than five miles per hour — they were creeping — yet even so, he felt the wheels sliding. He was helpless to stop the forward skidding motion even as he applied the brakes gently. He was shocked when the pickup suddenly stopped with a muffled grinding noise. At the same moment, the wall of snow opened, and the truck's lights shone out into the void above the deep canyon.

"What's happened?" Kim asked, her eyes wide with apprehension.

"I don't know," Tuck said, "I think we've run onto a mound of ice and snow."

He didn't want to tell her he thought the pickup was straddling a ridge of ice on the exposed drop-off side of the road, a berm of ice made when snowplow trucks from Orofino periodically scraped the road in winter.

Cautiously, Tuck put the pickup in reverse and slowly let the clutch out. The engine revved, the wheels spun and the pickup swayed. He tried moving the pickup forward with the same result. With sick dismay, Tuck realized the truck was centered on the upraised ice; the tires could not grip the surface hard enough to gain traction. He felt helpless, out of control.

"Tuck, what'll we do?" Kim whispered.

Tuck shook his head; he didn't want to admit, even to himself, how scared he was. Then, just as he was searching for an idea of how to dislodge the pickup, the truck lurched and dipped to the left, throwing Tuck against the driver's window. Kim, restrained like Tuck with a seatbelt, yelped. There was a moment of hesitation — it seemed like forever — then the pickup, with a rasping, grinding crunch, slid off the ice ridge and suddenly plunged.

"Help, we're going over, Tuck!" Kim grabbed for her boyfriend. Then the smashing, shuddering, hammering began as the pickup fell on its side with a bone-jarring jolt, turned over, landed on its roof and gouged chunks of snow, ice, frozen mud and rocks from the side of the mountain. Jammed behind the steering wheel in his seatbelt harness, He threw up his hands to protect his face from the broken glass as the windshield fractured, spraying Kim and Tuck with sharp cutting crystals.

Protecting himself from the shattered windshield was the last coherent thought Tuck had as the pickup rolled down the mountainside, accelerating, turning and twisting. As it gained momentum, the blows to the metal battered steel and flesh and stripped the tires from their crushed wheels.

To Tuck, as he prayed for a sudden, merciful death, the worst part of the falling terror was the pounding on his head and shoulders. The falling weight of the truck, as it crunched and bounced against the ground time after time, smashed and compressed the roof. He and Kim were like sardines trapped in a tin can that was being squeezed, dented and pummeled into an unrecognizable shape. Worst of all were the massive blows from the crunching roof shuddering through his body from the impact on his head and shoulders.

Dazed from the relentless pummeling, saved from being crushed against the steering wheel by the straps of his seat and shoulder belts, Tuck lost all sense of time. He was too confused to count the number of crunching revolutions in which the pickup wildly turned over 360 degrees as it plunged, struck, leaped in the air and smacked the mountainside. Tuck knew only that the awful ride would not stop until the broken and deformed pickup slammed to a halt at the bottom of the mountain where the Clearwater River flowed.

Only once or twice during the terrible descent did Tuck's glance fall on Kim who, like him, was strapped to her seat, moaning, crying and praying for deliverance.

When the pickup, having gathered sufficient downward momentum, hurtled clear of the mountain following a last smashing blow, it collided with a 100-foot ponderosa pine. The truck smashed into the tree forty feet above the ground, shaking the pine. For a moment, the pickup seemed to hang, grasping the trunk of the pine, then it dropped, drawing a long scar in the bark of the tree as it plunged. It landed at the foot of the tree, which was located on a narrow bench about two thousand feet from the bottom of the mountain.

The stillness at the bottom of the tree was like a blessing to Tuck. It took a moment or two for him to under-stand that he had survived; he was still alive. His voice came out in a croak when he answered Kim's screamed question, "Tuck, Tuck are you there? Get me out! Are you there?"

"I'm here, Kim. Hold on. Just hold on."

Tuck needed a few moments to collect himself, to marvel that he was still breathing. He knew that the truck's plunge down the mountain could not have taken longer than a minute, although it seemed as if an eternity separated them from his memory of trying to dislodge the teetering pickup from the ice ridge.

He discovered slowly that he could not breathe deeply. There was no pain in his chest, but he could not draw a full measure of air into his lungs. He was certain that he had suffered injuries and the adrenaline pumped by his body was protecting him from pain. Most noticeable was discomfort from his seatbelt; it was pulled tightly across his lap, cutting into his stomach and hips. That was the moment when he realized he was suspended upside down in the cab of the pickup, restrained by the lap belt and shoulder straps. Upside down he was, jammed into the crammed space under the steering wheel with part of the driver's seat stuffed with him against the floor of the truck.

"Tuck, get me out. Tuck! Tuck!"

Disturbed and frustrated by Kim's strident pleas, Tuck tried to reassure her. "I've got to get free, Kim. Hold on. It'll take a minute or two."

Tuck discovered that talking tired him, ate up his short breaths. Panic was closing in, aggravated by his helpless trapped-in-a-hole feeling, and he forced himself to take shallow sips of air. He was conscious that his scalp was wet: snow or blood? And he could move his head and shoulders, but one eye was blurry. Slowly, he figured out that the roof and hood of the pickup had been hammered to a level that was about equal to the height of the window sills. Also, a portion of the metal of the roof was jammed between the driver and passenger seats, creating a wall that separated him from Kim. The front lights of the pickup had been smashed in the fall down the mountain so the rare passing motorist up on the road above could not be alerted by the beams. As far as yelling for help was concerned, he was doubtful his voice would reach up the mountain, assuming anybody was around to hear it.

It was amazing they were alive.

Kim again raised her voice in a shrill cry for help, and he reassured her again, so that she subsided into a moaning reverie. Actually, in one fashion, Tuck was glad for Kim's hysteria. Her cries for help kept him awake; he so wanted to close his eyes, drift off to sleep. The drowsiness was not a good sign.

Tuck's inspection of his prison convinced him that the two of them had escaped death by a miracle. They were enclosed in a crumpled steel box, the only exit from which was a narrow hole — once the driver's window — filled with snow and dirt. It was located behind his head. By twisting his body he could claw free chunks of frozen sod and brush. The effort stole his breath, but he continued patiently, husbanding his air. He stopped when he felt cold air flow through the enlarged hole and said to Kim conversationally he thought he could get free. His everyday tone seemed to pacify her, and he spent the next five minutes probing with his fingers along the edges of the steel partition to locate the lap belt release button on the strap buckle. When he finally found it, he let out his breath with a sigh. He had not wanted to admit to himself how desperate he had been to find the key to his freedom. If it had been jammed just half an inch closer to Kim's seat, the steel partition would have buried it, and the two of them would have been helplessly trapped in a twisted steel tomb.

With the release of the lap belt Tuck felt blood flowing in his legs, and slowly he began to worm his way through the window hole he had cleared. When a few minutes later he crawled free of the cab into the snow at the base of the tree, he was confused. He estimated he had been hanging upside down for at least five minutes, and he felt disoriented. He wobbled to his feet and saw the vague lights of Orofino in the distance down the mountain. It was stormy and snow was falling up the mountain, dark, with streaks of night sky and stars peeking through running clouds. The night covered the tracks of the pickup's plunging trail down the mountain.

When Tuck edged around the front of the truck to Kim's side, he could reach in to touch her.

"Get me out, Tuck. Hurry, I'm scared," Kim cried.

Tuck was almost frantic when he removed his hand. It was covered with a warm, gooey, wet substance. God, he thought, she must be bleeding and in a bad way. Even without sufficient light for him to see her clearly, except for the blur of her white face, he knew she was trapped — held tightly in a steel embrace. With the crazy thought that he could turn the truck over to free Kim, Tuck strained to lift the upside-down machine, but gave up when the wreck refused to budge.

As he backed off, dropping his hands, gulping for air, something instinctual clicked in his mind — it was a deep infallible knowing that he couldn't waste time with foolish ideas and pointless effort. If Kim were to survive, he had to go for help; he had to leave her and climb the mountain. He had to get to the farmhouse perched back from the road, the one they'd passed with the merry Christmas lights shining in the window. It couldn't be more than a mile from the spot where the pickup had taken its dive.

As Tuck made his decision, he was aware that he was badly injured and if he hesitated much longer, he'd give in to the dreamy tide of lassitude that was creeping through his body, even though he felt sharp stabbing pains in his chest. The urge to lie down, curl up in the snow and sleep the night away was compelling.

Before he kneeled on Kim's side of the truck to tell her of his decision, he touched his wet face and ran his hands over his body. He discovered his hair was stiff with icicles — confirmation that the temperature was below freezing. Since he wormed his way out of the pickup, his injured right eye had closed. His breathing was even more shallow and rapid, and it was painful for him to lift his arms.

Kim was frantic at the idea that he would leave her alone. "You can't, Tuck. I'll die here. You can't leave me alone, you can't...."

"There's no other way, Kim, I've got to get help."

As he got to his feet, Tuck heard a hissing, popping sound and realized it was coming from the exposed muffler of the upended truck as snow and sleet dropped onto the heated metal. The horrifying thought that Kim might be in danger from seeping gasoline coming into contact with the super-hot exhaust system of the pickup made him hesitate. What if the truck blew up? Kim wouldn't have a chance.

"Tuck? Are you there Tuck?"

With a terrible, almost overpowering wave of guilt, Tuck said, "I'm going for help, Kim. It's the only way we're going to get you out."

Her lost weeping was a spur to Tuck as he started up the mountain. As he began climbing, he knew his reserve of strength was dwindling, and he made up his mind to ascend the steep slope in a direct line — to save time and energy. Pushing by shrubs, climbing over rocks, dodging small trees, and plunging his hands and feet into the snow to find grasping holds to pull his body up, he could not dismiss the heavy, sinking feeling that he was running away. He was leaving behind a helpless woman to die alone in a cold, steel coffin that might erupt at any moment in a blaze of gas and flames.

It was when Tuck had forced his way halfway up the steep incline and encountered the rockslide, an area dense with basketball-sized boulders, that he rested for a moment, considering whether to detour around the hazard. Aware of the sharp, throbbing pain in his neck and a scraping sound when he turned his head, he knew with a sick certainty that there was something awfully wrong with the bones at the top of his spine. His hands and fingers were numb; and his feet, clad in wool socks and low-topped dress shoes, were wet and without feeling.

Time was running out for him, and he still had half the mountain ahead. He fought down a wave of panic and stared up into the dark, trying to pierce the night with his uninjured eye and find the road. It was probably only a few seconds that he hesitated there gathering his strength, but it seemed like an age. It was at this moment, when the flame of life was flickering lowest in him, that Tuck felt the presence of an undefinable force which seemed to lift him with a message of deliverance: Rely on that which is greater than yourself. The silent words flooding through his heart gave him strength. He clenched his teeth and pushed himself forward foot by foot and bulldozed over the tops of the rocks. He moved in a daze, stumbling, sliding, bumping through the forest of bruising stones.

Twice the mountain moved as rounded boulders slipped under him, throwing him off balance, barking his knees and reversing his course. But he plowed ahead grimly, gasping for breath, straining for air, taking in small rapid gulps, unable to draw enough oxygen into his starving lungs.

In the next few minutes of climbing, time seemed to accelerate and, paradoxically, stand still. He imagined his dwindling strength was like the last few grains of sand disappearing in an hourglass. When at last he groped with his right hand and grasped an icy patch of hardened earth on the edge of the road above the drop-off, he shuddered with relief.

"I'm getting there," he said to Kim. "Hold on."

Grateful beyond words for the windswept, snow-crusted flat surface, Tuck covered the half-mile to the farm house swaying and stumbling down the center of the road. The Christmas lights were still bright in the front window.

Tuck barely remembered later the short distance to the back entrance of the house, or his knock on the door, which went unanswered, or how he found himself in a warm country kitchen looking out of his one eye at a teenaged girl whose face was frozen in an expression of dismay and fright when she took in the grotesque figure dripping blood and snow on the linoleum floor. Tuck had no idea how terrifying his appearance was to Jodi Richardson. She backed away, and Tuck followed.

Stumbling into the living room of the farmhouse with the Christmas tree dominating one corner, Tuck took in the surprised, wary faces of Jodi Richardson's mother, Karen; her brother, Daryl; and Jodi's uncle, who was holding a tray of cookies. He said to the man with the tray, "There's been an accident. My truck went off the road. My girlfriend's trapped."

At that moment, John Richardson walked through the kitchen into the living room. He had been in the barn checking on livestock when Tuck stumbled into the kitchen. With one encompassing glance at his visitor, he beckoned to his wife, Karen, and instructed his son, Daryl, to call a neighbor, "Tell Rick we've got a bad one down the hill, and to come on over."

"Let's get you into the kitchen," he said to Tuck, and with his arm around Tuck's shoulders, steered him to a chair.

The man who had put down the tray of cookies was John Richardson's brother, Bob. He knew better than to interfere with John when he went into action. Like his brother, he knew the most likely spot on the Gilbert Grade where the truck went off. More than one vehicle had plunged to the bottom from the unguarded road.

Karen Richardson knew exactly what to do for Tuck. With experienced calm, she instructed her daughter, Jodi, to fetch a blanket while she poured coffee for Tuck — a stimulant to get his blood moving, she said. And she helped him hold the steaming cup to his lips. She was afraid to clean up his head after she tucked a blanket around his shoulders. She was concerned that the cap of blood, pine needles, and melting ice concealed serious injuries. When her husband and son, coated for the weather and equipped with ropes and flashlights, were joined by Rick Miller, the neighbor from next door, she barely acknowledged their departure and said to Tuck, "Now, don't you worry. Rick is the foreman of the Clearwater County Emergency Medical Team. Between him and my husband, if your friend's alive, she's in good hands. An ambulance is on the way to pick you up. My, you've had quite a night. It seems like somebody's looking out for you."

The next hour was hazy, unreal and frightening for Tuck as he slipped in and out of consciousness, convinced, in his waking moments, that Kim was probably dead and it was his fault, hoping he was wrong. It was through a confused blur of pain that he discovered two strange faces bent over him as he lay on his back on the kitchen floor, fighting for breath. How did he get on his back?

It was the pain, like sharp knives sticking in his ribs and the terrible clutching feeling in his chest, robbing him of air, that brought him around. He heard a voice say, "His chest's a mess. We'd better prop him up or he'll drown in his own blood."

Tuck panicked for a moment when they clamped a mask over his mouth and nose and lifted him on a stretcher; then he was grateful, and he was crying with relief as cold, clean oxygen pumped into his lungs.

Tuck Miller did not learn about the rescue of Kim Jude until almost five in the morning the day after Christmas. He was brought into the emergency room of the

Clearwater County Hospital about ten o'clock the night before, and there physicians began repairing Tuck's body. For a deep gash below his right eye, eight stitches were taken. His right ear, almost torn from the side of his face, and swollen to three times its normal size, required a dozen stitches. Every rib on the right side of his chest had been ripped from his sternum — the sturdy, flat bone bisecting the middle of the chest — and forced into the chest cavity, piercing and collapsing his right lung. The two clavicle bones, which stabilize the shoulders, were ripped out of the sterna-clavicular joints, accounting for the fact that for weeks Tuck could not lift his arms above the height of his shoulders without excruciating pain. The only broken bone in his body was the first right rib, located high in the chest under the right clavicle. On top of these injuries, Tuck suffered from a concussion, ripped muscles and grievous soft tissue injuries. Much later, physicians would discover that a disc in his neck had ruptured, and an interior diskectomy with iliac bone graft fusion would be performed. A dowel-shaped piece of bone taken from his hip would be used to replace the crushed disk in his spine. The grating noise in his neck Tuck heard when he was climbing the mountain was the disk crackling in the vertebrae

During the repair of his body, as he faded in and out of consciousness, Tuck listened in on the emergency room radio to the progress of the rescue efforts to extricate Kim Jude. Repeatedly, he asked about her condition. And when, routinely, he was informed that men were still trying to get her out, he became morose, convinced that the medical attendants were shielding him from her death.

He sank back against his pillow, certain that he had failed. Kim had died alone, crying for help. His climb up the mountain had been for nothing.

It was when he awoke from a troubled sleep that he saw Kim lying on a gurney a few feet away from him in the emergency room. A thick black coating of blood plastering her hair to her face and covering her head and the useless cervical collar that held her neck in place were proof that she had not survived. He was confused, and his heart leaped when he heard her whisper, "Is that you, Tuck? I can't turn my head."

Tuck learned later that John Richardson and his neighbor, Rick Miller, the foreman of the Clearwater County Emergency Medical Team, had rappelled down the side of the mountain, leaving Richardson's son, Daryl, 20, a college student home for Christmas vacation, to stand on the Gilbert Grade to relay signals from his father to the sheriff's search and rescue team when it arrived at the departure site of the pickup from the road.

Richardson and Miller, reaching Kim quickly, discovered she was alive but so imprisoned by the compressed wreckage of the pickup that it was impossible to release her. So tightly was she jammed into the twisted metal that they were unable to wrap a warming blanket around her. An oddity of the situation was the mistaken film of blood covering every inch of her hair, head and neck. Not blood at all, the rescuers learned, but oil dripping from the broken crankcase of the motor. Thick, viscous liquid formed a protective layer on her skin, hair, neck and shoulders, a thermal barrier to the wind and cold. Except for a broken neck, there wasn't a scratch on Kim's body. Strangely, the vise of steel that held her as an unmovable captive also supported her head and spine in such a remarkable fashion that she was saved from death. The vulnerable C-2 vertebrae in her spine had ruptured. Had she been able to turn her head, the motion surely would have punctured her spinal cord — the outcome being death or permanent paralysis from the neck down. Kim was extricated from the compressed pickup four hours after Richardson and Miller arrived. Recognizing the perils of removing her, they spoke words of encouragement and told her how Tuck had climbed the mountain. A call was placed to the search and rescue team from Nez Perce, Idaho, twenty miles away. The response was quick, and the team from the neighboring town arrived with inflatable bags and steel "Jaws of Life."

The first step of the combined rescuers, coordinated by Clearwater County Deputy Sheriff Nick Albers, was to carefully secure the upended pickup to the pine tree with ropes. Albers was concerned the wreck was lying too close to the edge of the mountain bench to which the pine tree clung. It was only twenty feet wide. Below it was a fall of two thousand feet.

Next, the men inflated the thick rubber bags brought from Nez Perce after digging a space for them under the pickup. When filled with air, the bags lifted the pickup off the ground, allowing room for the men with the "Jaws of Life" to place the steel expanders into the caved-in window of the truck. It was from this enlarged space that Kim Jude was maneuvered cautiously after medics applied a surgical collar to keep her broken neck in a safe position.

An hour later, she was swung up to the Gilbert Grade via a pulley-operated lifeline attached from the pine tree to a rescue vehicle on the road.

One of the visitors to call on Tuck two days after he was brought to the Clearwater County Hospital was Nick Albers. The stocky deputy sheriff extended his hand to Tuck and said with a smile and a shake of his head, "I just had to meet somebody who could live through something like that. Your pickup looks like one of those big bundles of scrap you see on the back of trucks after they've been through the car crusher. You got any idea how lucky you are?"

Nick Albers' question was one that occupied Tuck Miller's mind for weeks as he recuperated and after he returned to biathlon competition following the anterior diskectomy operation. Despite his extensive injuries, his robust good health and excellent physical condition at the time of the accident aided his quick recovery. Kim, on the other hand, went through a series of neurosurgical operations to restore her broken neck. She was flown to Boise, Idaho, by helicopter shortly after physicians examined her at Clearwater County Hospital in Orofino. A physician who studied Tuck's injury list after he had been discharged from the hospital, particularly the damage recorded to his chest, lungs and spine, concluded that Tuck should not have been able to climb the mountain.

With the injuries he sustained, the minute he stood on his feet after he got out of the wreck he should have been incapacitated by lack of oxygen. Nobody, no matter how superb his physical condition, could climb a mountain with his lungs filled with blood, the ends of his ribs sticking like knives into the chest cavity. Even, say, he could do the unimaginable and barge up the mountain with scant oxygen to breathe, how could he pull himself 600 feet up a thirty-five-degree grade with both clavicle bones completely dislocated? They'd been forced inward, torn from their integuments. The clavicles are the stabilizers for the whole complex of muscles in the shoulders. Without them...? Inconceivable! And the pain? Excruciating.

Yet with these injuries, neck-bones grating with every step, and a concussion of the brain, defying all medical logic, Tuck Miller did on a freezing Christmas Night, 1988, climb the mountainside to the Gilbert Grade where he stumbled half a mile to the John Richardson farmhouse.

Eight years after his heroic adventure, Tuck reflected on his nightmare and concluded that "something, somebody, was looking out for me. I've talked to athletes like me who say they've been in the zone where they seem to perform above themselves, where they're superior to their bodies. I don't know, maybe I was in the zone that Christmas Day. I think it was a test for me. Before then, I'd never thought much about God, or any external force, but after that day, I knew I was being saved for something in life ... I don't know what it is and it doesn't matter; it's there and it was present when I climbed the mountain."

The most unforgivable thing a writer can do is to attribute misleading words or unintended meaning to a person who has been interviewed. It happens quite frequently, and that is unfortunate. But it does seem apparent that Tuck Miller was the recipient of unusual power on Christmas Day 1988. Examining his case, relying on the medical evidence of his injuries, the eyewitness reports of the Richardsons, and his own description of his trial, it appears Tuck's strong motivation to save Kim may have provided the impetus for him to integrate mind, body and spirit and overcome the obstacles of his injuries to climb the mountain.

From Tuck's narrative, the reader must decide about the nature of his inspiration; and was his physical performance an example of the unity of mind, body and spirit that hundreds of athletes have described in their personal fashion? We know that athletes and many others have experienced sustained energy bursts; and they know, as many sports scientists have discovered, that expending energy can generate higher levels of force.

It is this energy — which athletes and others described in this book have experienced, sought after, gloried in and tried successfully and unsuccessfully to repeat — that is the chief subject of the authors' inquiry. But our interest goes beyond defining the mystery of this energy; it embraces the promise in the application of this energy to the expanding horizon of human development. We are convinced that people are poised on the threshold of discovering powers within them which are beyond imagining — superlative powers of mind, body and spirit which authors Oscar Ratti and Adde Westbrook referred to in their book, *Secrets of the Samurai,* as "far more encompassing and comprehensive in both substance and intensity than the common type of energy usually associated with the output of man's muscular system alone."

2

Interaction of Mind, Body and Spirit

Chapter Two offers the reader personal experiences showing that we humans are far more than we think. Athletes and others who have reached beyond themselves into the zone utilize extraordinary powers of mind, body and spirit in unity, portraying the true potential of man.

In recorded history there has never been a culture that did not believe in a unity of the three dimensions: body, mind and spirit. It seems logical that to fully explore the outreaches of human performance, we must understand how these three components interact.

To demonstrate a whol(e)istic method of achieving improved personal performance — a method that integrates the three aspects of self — we have asked champion performers how they brought together mind, body and spirit, and if they believe such a unified approach is the optimal way to view human capability.

We support the notion in this chapter that viewing the ultimate self without limitations is the result of learning to blend the power of the union of the three selves.

Consider the idea of running confidently for the high jump and sailing over the bar set at a vertical height of nine feet.

Imagine possessing the remarkable strength that Tuck Miller displayed on Christmas Night, 1988. Or what about calmly lifting the front end of a 4,000-pound automobile to save a trapped child?

Are the physical accomplishments described above figments of the imagination, ideas impossible of achieving, or are they athletic feats which someday may come to pass? Was Tuck Miller's remarkable climb up a mountain one of those freak happenings that does not merit serious consideration?

We are capable of far more than we realize when body, mind and spirit are synchronized in pursuit of a single objective. And that statement partially expresses the purpose of this book: To demonstrate how remarkable feats which seem to defy explanation are merely examples of the awesome human potential each one of us is capable of tapping into, but from which we bar ourselves because of our timidity, ignorance and closedmindedness. Rather than believe we are powerful individuals, vivid participants in the energy of the universe, expressed in the beauty of individuality replicated millions of times to create a community of life, we choose to reject that which we cannot understand.

But the fact is that sports, requiring, as they do, intense effort, energy and endurance on the part of the

athlete, often lead the player into extraordinary performances characterized by mystical feelings, strange sensa-
tions and altered perceptions. These experiences are like
those of persons who meditate deeply to release themselves
to come in contact with the benign power of the universe.
Sports people who reach a sense of elevated well-being
while they are performing at their absolute best have
reported moments of mystery and awe, invincibility, a unity
with all things, and a feeling of immortality. Addressing his
own experience of the mystical, physician-runner George
Sheehan wrote in *Runners' World:* "That first thirty minutes
[of running] is for my body. During that half-hour, I take joy
in my physical ability, the endurance and power of my
running. I find it a time when I feel myself competent and
in control of my body, when I can think about my problems
and plan my day-to-day world. In many ways, that thirty
minutes is all ego, all the self. It has to do with me, the individual.

"What lies beyond this fitness of muscle? I can only
answer for myself. The next thirty minutes is for my soul.
In it, I come upon the third wind (unlike the second wind,
which is physiological). And then I see myself not as an
individual but as part of the universe. In it, I can happen
upon anything I ever read or saw or experienced. Every fact
and instinct and emotion is unlocked and made available to
me through some mysterious operation in my brain."

And so in this book we bring you athletes who have
performed feats of strength and have entered out-of-body
experiences, not because they are strange or mystical, but
because we believe, as many others do, that they reflect the
power and mystery available to each one of us. But we are
sorely afraid to identify that power and mystery as part of
ourselves. To do so would mean that our potential is beyond

comprehension and would require a basic shift in our whole belief system, in how we view ourselves, the world, and the universe beyond.

Expanding on this last assertion, we have come up with the following definition of the benefits a reader may expect from what we have written: You will learn how to achieve a high level of personal excellence from exemplary athletes who have become champions in sports and in the art of living. Through interviews and vivid anecdotes, uplifting stories of personal struggle and triumph emerge. There is Bob Richards, champion pole-vaulter, Olympic gold medalist, and first athlete on the Wheaties box; Stacy Allison, the first American woman to climb Mount Everest; Lanny Bassham, Olympic gold medalist rifle shooter; and Marilyn King, the pentathlete with an injured back who visualized with amazing accuracy exactly how she would win her Olympic trials. These four, and more than thirty other champions profiled in this book have provided inspirational narratives substantiating the fact that all of us can increase remarkably our performance in life through the integration of body, mind and spirit.

The stories of the men and women we've interviewed are marvelous and in themselves make the book worth treasuring, but our underlying motive is to show you — through them — how to arrive at an enlarged, more joyous and empowering image of yourself.

We chose to write about the experiences of athletes connecting body, mind and spirit in performance because in a very true sense, the physical exertions, willpower and endurance required of athletes often place them in a near-meditative state called the zone.

Basketball player Patsy Neal described the zone — the integration of body, mind and spirit — in her book *Sport and Identity* when she wrote: "There are moments of glory that go beyond the human expectation, beyond the physical and emotional ability of the individual. Something unexplainable takes over and breathes life into the known life. One stands on the threshold of miracles that one cannot create voluntarily ... call it a state of grace, or an act of faith ... or an act of God. It is there and the impossible becomes possible ... the athlete goes beyond herself; she transcends the natural. She touches a piece of heaven and becomes the recipient of power from an unknown source.

"The power goes beyond that which can be defined as physical or mental. The performance almost becomes a holy place — where a spiritual awakening seems to take place. The individual becomes swept up in the action around her — she almost floats through the performance, drawing on forces she has never previously been aware of."

Many athletes who have experienced an exalted state, as Patsy Neal described, deny that its derivation may be "a state of grace, or an act of faith ... or an act of God." As a matter of fact, as we discovered in our interviews with top athletes, when the subject of melding body, mind and spirit came up, a few of them were shy or awkward about discussing the idea of calling on God or an external source for assistance in their performances. In the majority of cases, the reluctance to attribute increased performance to a spiritual component added to the mind-body combination was not because they found the idea difficult, but merely because they hadn't thought about it deeply.

Notwithstanding the reluctance of some athletes to probe their psyches in search of the "spiritual" key to extraordinary performance, sports medicine scientists are convinced that amazing athletic feats are within reach if individuals can unlock the door to the secret power in their bodies.

What is the combination that can make athletes utilize 100 percent of their potential? How can they learn to perform above themselves? How does the development of superior athletic performance benefit those of us who are spectators, who admire a smashing return over the net, the thirty-yard run to a touchdown, the breathtaking long jump that breaks the world record? There are some intriguing answers to these questions, but none more fascinating than the comments of Dr. C. Etta Walters, who for years was associated with the Florida State University Institute of Human Development. A pioneer and researcher on aspects of sports medicine, Dr. Walters observed more than thirty years ago that, "We don't even know what 100 percent of potential means. We know that human performance, sports performance, can exceed what's been demonstrated so far. But we shy away from investigating a synergy of mind, body and spirit that can accomplish what we often refer to as 'miracles.'"

The miracles Dr. Walters spoke of are dramatic incidents when ordinary people perform extraordinary accomplishments, like effortlessly lifting a heavy automobile. As Dr. Walters explained to one of the authors of this book, the seat of extraordinary power, she believed, lies in the "Great Arousal Center," GAC, located in the brain stem. When fear, excitement or extreme desire spurs a person to action, the GAC, she theorized, operates as a power plant, bombarding the necessary muscles to perform a physical act with excited motor neurons. Simultaneously, the GAC short-circuits normal inhibitions and the body responds with a single purpose.

"The problem we are trying to solve is to find a way for athletes to short-circuit normal inhibitions voluntarily," said Dr. Walters.

Research into the secret of the Great Arousal Center in the brain led Dr. Walters to investigate amazing feats of strength such as that demonstrated by Charles Dennis Jones in October, 1952. Jones, a six-foot-two-inch tire changer for Robertson Transport of Houston, Texas, appeared suddenly at the scene of a terrible accident in which Roy Gaby, a Houston, Texas, trucker driving a heavy fourteen-wheeled truck-trailer swerved to avoid a drunk driver. Gaby's truck smashed into a mammoth oak tree, trapping him in the twisted, crumpled cab.

Efforts of wreckers to "untelescope" the cab in which Gaby was imprisoned — pulling the accordioned metal apart with two trucks linked together in a chain of power — were futile. Worse, flames spurted from beneath the truck, threatening Gaby with a horrible death. No extinguisher was on hand to smother the growing fire. The fire engines and emergency equipment on their way to the accident had not arrived yet and they might be too late. That was the moment, with the flames inching toward Gaby, when a husky black man, Charles Dennis Jones arrived.

Taking in the danger to Gaby at a glance, Jones strode to the cab, placed his sturdy hands on the wrinkled door, and wrenched it free. He accomplished in a few seconds what two tow trucks could not do. Breathless with fascination, the crowd which had gathered watched as Jones, solemn and glacially calm, reached into the cab, whipped out the burning floor mat, smothered the flames with his big hands, then wiggled into the cab and assumed a squatting position. That was the crucial moment, with his neck and shoulders braced against the crushed roof of the cab, that a man in the crowd said in an awed whisper, "Why, that guy's not calm, he's mad as hell!" A woman screamed, "Look, he's pushing up the top like it was paper!"

Muscles bulging, the metal of the cab screeching as it gave way, Jones forced the top up. With his body quivering, he held his position until rescuers pulled Gaby free. In the excitement of the trucker's release, Jones slipped away without anybody discovering his name.

It wasn't until the next day that Jones' identity was revealed. When he was asked by newspaper reporters how he had summoned the remarkable strength to wrench off the heavy steel door and prop up the crumpled steel roof, he said, "A man don't know what he can do until another man is hurting."

Dozens of men and women have, like Jones, demonstrated remarkable feats of strength. But how, Dr. Walters asked, could athletes place themselves in a frame of mind that would call upon the Great Arousal Center to inspire superior performances? It was clear to Dr. Walters from her observations that ordinary people who perform miraculous feats of strength — Charles Dennis Jones wrenching a steel door from its hinges, Tuck Miller climbing the mountain — were deeply motivated by fear, anger or the threat of loss. These emotions acted as precipitating factors to engage the GAC. In turn, the GAC flooded the body with the synergy of enhanced muscular strength, emotional direction and physical power which enabled a mobilized individual to perform far above his normal ability.

The state into which Charles Dennis Jones entered is similar, Dr. Walters observed, to those, perhaps less dramatic, but equally valid experiences, described by Shane Murphy. Murphy, a sports psychologist, consulted with Olympic hopefuls at the United States Olympic Training Center in Colorado Springs from 1987 to 1994. An athlete himself who has experienced the zone, Murphy in 1994 circulated an informal survey to 100 athletes involved in many different sports, asking the question: "Can you get into the zone?"

Ninety percent of the athletes said "Yes, I can get into it." They affirmed that they could access the power available to everybody when they entered the special timeless, measureless space-energy continuum which has come to be called "the zone" or "the flow."

In his own case, Murphy, a native of Australia, described what happened to him as a fifteen-year-old who was plunged into the zone when the tennis team in which he was playing was challenged by rivals who belittled Murphy and his co-players. "We got mad. There were six of us and we were top-seeded, the number one team going in. But as so often happens, we were nervous when we went out, and we got clobbered the first two sets.

"I'm sure if the match had continued right then, we would have lost, but there was a thunderstorm and we had to recess for about an hour to allow it to go by. While we were waiting, we overheard the other team ridiculing us and bragging about how they were going to take the district championship trophy home with them.

"Bill, one of the quiet members of our team, just got furious. He was burning when he said, 'That's our trophy they're talking about. Let's show them.'

"Well, when we got back on the courts, we clobbered them. It was amazing. There was nothing we could do wrong. I did things with the ball you only dream about, and never repeated. We were like dancers in a ballet, rising and dipping, stroking and striking as if our eyes and arms were guided in a marvelous synchrony. We definitely were in the zone, as I've come to understand it from other athletes who've been there."

Daisetz Suzuki, in his book *Zen and the Japanese Culture,* explained that when thinking interferes with a task, you have to leave it behind, as was probably the case, Shane Murphy affirmed, when his tennis team exploded into the zone. "It is a non-thinking series of moments," he said.

Suzuki wrote, "In such cases you cease to be your own conscious master but become an instrument in the hands of the unknown. The unknown has no ego-consciousness, and consequently no thought of winning the contest.... It is for this reason that the sword [wielded by great fencing masters] moves where it ought to move and makes the contest end victoriously. This is the practical application of the Lao Tzuan doctrine of 'doing by not doing.'"

Taking purpose from observations like those of Suzuki, sports medicine researchers and sports psychologists, like Shane Murphy and Walters earlier, have concluded that the athlete who transcends his own achievements, his own records, does so when he frees himself of all ideas of gain and loss, right and wrong, giving himself up to the power which lives deeply in his inner being.

"We perform best when we think the least," Dr. Walters observed, pointing out that famous pistol marksmen of the Western frontier, gunslingers, were able to draw, aim and shoot in one swift motion with unbelievable accuracy. They were able to unerringly hit their target because their gun hand was controlled by an internal coordination so exquisitely exacting that the action was like lightning flashing along a pre-established groove. The "inner eye" zeroed in on the target and directed the thrust of the pistol, aiming, and trigger sequence in a nerveless arch of precision.

This precision was addressed by Lawrence Shainberg in a *New York Times Magazine* article, a portion of which addressed the manner in which champion archers are able to free themselves from volition and thought and, like the gunslinger of old, from consciousness itself when they release their arrows.

Said Shainberg, "Then, too, there is the matter of releasing the arrow, which ... must not be an act of decision or will. The great enemy for an archer, as perhaps for any athlete, is conscious intervention. [The] conscious mind always wants to help you, but usually it messes you up. But you can't just set it aside, you've got to get it involved. The thing you have to do is anchor it in technique. Then your unconscious mind, working with your motor memory, will take over the shooting for you."

As we noted, some athletes resist the idea of consciously drawing on the "spirit" to improve their performance. Their resistance, we believe, stems from a mistaken sense of trespassing into forbidden territory — an area of the spiritual proscribed as the exclusive domain of formal religion. They may have been trained in church to believe in a narrow definition of God. To experiment with "spirit," which is often defined as the body of belief in Christ, is to tread on sacred truths. Many athletes who have had "deep flow" experiences resist definitions like the "eternal moment," even though they admit to being lost in a total absorption event which entirely consumed their mind, body and soul as if the winds of eternity were blowing through their expanded being.

It was Bob Richards, the first man in the world to win Olympic gold by clearing fifteen feet in the pole-vault, who presented us with his view of the spiritual aspects of remarkable performance. He made it plain that the "force of God — the spirit" — was the extra wind that lifted him to victory in sports and in life.

For Bob Richards, as a *Sports Illustrated* article pointed out, the world of sports has no room for backsliders or men of faint spirit. "Not only do Richards' athletes remember to say their prayers, they advance into battle enduring torturous injuries. Runners tear ashen-faced down the stretch while others are popping up, one after another, from operating tables to plunge into training against terrible odds."

Richards does admire men and women who seem to have wills of iron, and perhaps his reverence for toughness on the playing field was the inspiration for his own painful trial in Finland. At Helsinki, scene of guts and gumption at the 1952 Olympics, the Reverend Bob, with pain running through his left leg like a sword of fire, pounded down the runway and soared to an Olympic pole-vault record. His own example may have been a match for contestants who seem to spit in the eye of medical science and perform feats of physical endurance and torture that must be inspired, he believes, by the breath of God.

Nine years before he won the gold in Helsinki, Bob Richards was a dirty-faced, sixteen-year-old delinquent running the streets of Champaign, Illinois, the head of a street gang, drinking whisky in back alleys, stealing from stores. Since the police were looking for the gang, Bob spent much of the daytime hiding out in a friend's apartment.

It was the girl he'd been dating who begged him to reform. One evening she convinced him to visit the jovial Reverend Merlin Garber, a minister of the Church of the Brethren. Talking with Bob, the Reverend Garber learned that the boy had no home, his parents were not together and, like a wild animal, forsaken and dusty, he'd been running the streets, living by his wits.

Behind the grime, the Reverend Garber thought he saw something fine in Bob Richards.

Bob was impressed by Garber, and it wasn't difficult for the minister to convince him to move in. The house was a clean, quiet home with good, warm food; and before he knew it Bob began attending high school again and quit the gang. A few months later five members of the gang were caught stealing and ended up in jail.

After school Bob sat with the Reverend Garber, fascinated by passages read to him by the minister from the bible. At school he focused his wild energy on sports, and at Champaign High he became quarterback on the football team and soon was the state's third-best pole-vaulter. One day Bob said to the Reverend Garber, "Do you think I could find a place in religion?"

"It's something only you can say," said the sympathetic minister. "Forget everything that happened before we met," he advised. "Consider only how close you feel to God."

It wasn't much later that Bob decided to go to Bridgewater College in Virginia, a Church of the Brethren school, to study theology. This was his first step toward becoming a minister. There he met Mary Cline, the woman he would marry.

At Bridgewater, Bob began to win pole-vaulting championships. Once he soared thirteen and one-half feet, but he was far from satisfied. One day he took a friend aside and confided, "I'm going to leap fifteen feet someday."Forget everything that happened before we met,Warmerdam — and that was ten years ago," his friend reminded him.

"I'll do it," said Richards.

Bob seemed to have reached his goal in 1950, at the Millrose games in New York. There, he raced down the board runway, floated high into the air, sailing over the bar.

He jumped up, waving to the crowd enthusiastically as the announcer's voice boomed: "Fifteen feet! Bob Richards has cleared fifteen feet!"

Bob's joy was dashed when the officials announced that there had been a mistake. The setting of the bar was wrong, a half-inch below fifteen feet. Disappointed, Bob returned home to Laverne, California, where he was teaching at a small college. There he made a solemn promise to himself: "Someday I will clear fifteen feet. I know the answer is inside me."

A year later, on the night of January 27, 1951, at the same Millrose games, Bob demonstrated his faith in himself. His muscular arms pushed his wiry five-foot-ten, 160-pound body high into the air, swinging over the bar at fifteen feet, one inch! This time there was no mistake.

By 1952, on his way to Helsinki for the Olympics, Bob had cleared the magic mark more than two dozen times, and now he had another goal; to be the first to soar fifteen feet in the air at the Olympic games in front of a crowd of thousands.

But, like the wounded athletes he had admired and who persevered, Bob was stricken with a pulled muscle in his left leg just a few days before the Olympics were to start. For days he couldn't vault.

"It's like a knife sticking in the back of my leg," he told coach Brutus Hamilton.

On a cool July day in the Helsinki stadium, Bob was on the field when the Olympic pole vaulting began. Biting his lip, trying to erase the pain from his mind, he jumped fourteen feet, one inch; then fourteen feet, five inches, an Olympic record; then fourteen feet, nine inches. The bar was set at fourteen feet, eleven and one-eighth inches, with only Bob and his teammate, Don Laz, left in the competition.

On his try, Laz missed all three times; Bob missed twice.

Finally, on his third and last leap, with the bar set at fifteen feet, Bob faced the fact that if he missed on this trial, Laz would be the winner. His partner had scored fewer misses for the whole competition.

This was the moment when Bob, standing on the runway, head down, asked God to help him.

"I didn't ask God to give me a win, just a boost. I remember saying, 'Anything you can do, Lord, I'll appreciate.'"

The next moments were dramatic on the playing field.

"On reflection," Bob said, "there was a change in the air I couldn't explain, but the emotional excitement in the arena died down, the tightness and tension left me … the crossbar began to come down to fifteen feet in my mind where it belonged … I took off."

Down the runway he charged, the pole sticking straight out in front of him, like the salient of a knight, his eyes fixed on the slot in the ground into which he'd jam the bamboo.

There was the slot!

Bob soared, up toward the crossbar that hung between him and the sky and an Olympic gold medal. "And that was the instant," Bob said, "when I felt an invisible hand push me up and over, as if by an extension of my own will."

As he climbed, feeling lifted by the force he'd called on, Bob pushed down on the pole, his body jackknifing over the bar. Then he threw the pole away, turning and twisting at the same time, pulling in his chest and pulling his arms back away from the bar.

Down he came, his face straining upward, watching the bar. He struck the sawdust pit, jumped to his feet, looked up, saw the crossbar still stationary on its pegs and, as he said, "I could have gone over that crossbar again — this time without a pole."

Down the track he ran, limping, shouting at the crowd, which was standing and cheering him. Later, in the dressing room, he told reporters, "Four days ago I was about ready to quit. What I found was what a lot of champions have discovered — that when you've given everything, there's something else you can call on. I don't know what you call it, but for me it's God."

Reflecting on his first Olympic gold medal win (he won a second gold medal in the pole-vault four years later in 1956), Bob said, "No, God didn't hold Don Laz down so I could win. But he responded within my subconscious, within my spiritual chakra; he told me what I had to do to be my best. Now that's the way I put prayer in the light."

Bob said that, for him, "getting into the zone" means asking God to help him by coming into every cell he owns. "Most people," he said, "have all kinds of negative thoughts, and I call this short-circuiting. They short-circuit their whole being. They start to do something great and say, well, I can't do that. Or, somebody won't like this or that. It's a short-circuit. But, if you have synchronism — mind, body and spirit in harmony — when every cell, like Jack London said, when every atom is magnetic and magnificent, you're synchronized. You are in harmony with yourself. You are not short-circuiting. You are not full of negative thoughts. You are saying, 'I can do it. I'm made in God's image. God made me for greatness, and I deserve great things to happen to me.'"

"Do you hear what I'm saying? There's a whole mental image that goes with this biblical thing of trusting God and believing that he wants you to do great things with your life. Not that he's going to hold other people down."

We asked Bob Richards some questions about synchronizing mind, body and spirit after explaining the GAC theory of Professor Etta Walters. Did he think, we asked, if what she described came from the same source as his inspiration at Helsinki in 1952.

Bob said, "I think now you have really hit upon something. From a scientific point of view, what they have done with hypnosis in many areas corroborates this spiritual thing that I have been talking about. For example, take the great runner Joan Benoit, who, six weeks after a knee operation, goes into the marathon in the Los Angeles Olympics. Did you see her face? They kept showing her face through that whole marathon. What was incredible about it, I swear, is that every time I saw her straining face cast in determination (you know she ran through smog and heat that was unbearable), you just knew that if she had thought like any ordinary person would have in those adverse circumstances, she never would have been able to do what she did. But looking at her eyes, she appeared hypnotized. She must have said to herself, 'Here's the pace I want to run. I'm going to do it, regardless. I'm not going to back off.'"

Addressing himself to the idea of the Great Arousal Center, Bob theorized that people who pick up 2,000-pound cars are calling on an inner power potential, power that is there all the time. "I guess what I'm trying to get at is that there is a hidden potential that we know nothing of, and that only comes out in very freakish or unusual situations. And that's why I think that parapsychology and other esoteric investigations are getting at stuff that is just beyond what we have done before. But that doesn't mean it can't happen. There's much more to all of this."

Bob made the point that, when a person orients his mind around great thoughts, thoughts of being like God, being part of God, doing what God wants a person to do, then universal power coordinates normal human responses to go to the ultimate.

"Some athletes call it the zone," Bob said, "but the power is much bigger than that."

We asked Bob if he believed that training alone would produce the same effects as training while engaging the whole divine light in the process.

He answered by referring to the great philosopher Schopenhauer, who said, "Will is the most important thing in a human being." Then he observed, as if awed by memory, "I think will is demonstrated when I watch Tom Courtney about to pass out in Melbourne, Australia, and Johnson of Great Britain goes racing by him. Then Courtney, with some superhuman will-power, forces himself to start sprinting, although his legs are completely gone. He comes back the last sixty or seventy yards, dives into the tape, and beats Johnson by three or four inches. Then, he passes out for two hours. They have to delay the victory ceremony for him to come to.

"Now, that's running down to the last red corpuscle you've got! That is willpower. Maybe it's being in the zone. We speak about the intangible — something we know so little about. Well, how can you be in athletics and not see and feel this unbelievable willpower? It has to have a foundation that is deeper than the muscles, deeper than the brain. It is the potential that every human has to learn how to let out. And it isn't magical, and it isn't non-scientific. It's very scientific. Ultimately we will find out how it all collaborates."

Few among the athletes we talked with were unfamiliar with "the zone." This term was "safe" to them, uncontroversial, and it was non-exclusive of the higher power to which Bob Richards referred. Also, we discovered that anthropologically, psychologically, neurologically and biologically, the zone has been related by investigators — as Shainberg wrote in his *New York Times Magazine* article — "To hypnosis, spiritual or martial arts practice and parapsychology; and ascribed to genetics, environment and motivation, not to mention skill. On the negative side, statisticians have offered studies which demonstrate, they say, that many 'streaks' in sports are no more unusual than streaks in gambling or a long run of coin-tossing, and some neuroscientists have called the heightened perception reported by players like Ted Williams a sort of illusion or even hallucination."

Many investigators, we believe, are intransigent when it comes to defending a rock-like personal viewpoint of the world as non-shifting, dependable, ruled by definable laws and logic that reject spirituality as unmeasurable, untouchable, invisible and, therefore, unsubstantial and even fraudulent.

The evidence, however, speaks for a broader, more enlightened view. We've come to the conclusion that it doesn't make any difference whether or not an athlete, or anybody who finds himself in the zone, expresses the power that comes from it as the source of divine energy. It really doesn't matter! The power exists for all of us to explore and use. It doesn't require definition, recognition or praise. It merely is, like an endless, inexhaustible river without boundaries or time.

Anyone who has learned how may dip into the flow to expand his own concept of himself and magnify his body and mental powers. All of the athletes we've interviewed for this book have demonstrated magnified power. Each in his own way has reaffirmed Michael Murphy and Rhea White when they wrote: "The body is not the end of sport, but its beginning. It is a centering point, a place to start from, but from this sturdy base we are capable of reaching beyond — of fleshing our spirit in areas where the body cannot reach, initiating movements the eye cannot see, revealing strengths that transcend muscles, exerting energies that are not physical in the ordinary sense. Sport is not merely an end in itself, but a catalyst for human enfoldment in other areas in life."

Chris Campbell, lawyer, father, world-champion wrestler, and Olympic bronze medalist, asserts that his sport was the catalyst for his personal human enfoldment.

Campbell, a man who has wrestled with one form of adversity or another most of his life, was reared by three women — his mother, Margery; his grandmother, Odell; and his aunt, Gladys — in a poor section of Westfield, New Jersey. Chris bagged groceries, delivered papers and pumped gas after school to help with the family budget.

"My mother cleaned houses and struggled to put food on the table every week," he reflected.

Trouble in school during his early years seemed to end in fights every day, Campbell said. Preoccupied with his "attitude," with defending himself, and with problems at home, Campbell did so poorly that he was forced to repeat the fourth grade. He attributed his poor showing to his mother's difficulty with being a single parent whose husband had deserted her long before. Her problems seemed to disappear after she became a Jehovah's Witness.

Of this event in her life, Chris said, "My mother seemed to come to terms with her life and started to be a very positive influence. By the seventh grade, I made the honor roll."

That was when Chris discovered wrestling. "I saw some guys wrestle at a high school match," he said. "I was fascinated because they were doing all those complicated moves. It looked like a dance almost."

Chris found himself and quickly mastered the steps, becoming undefeated during his high school years. So taken by the sport was he that he sold his car for $100 to finance a trip to the University of Iowa, then — as now — the top of the mountain of American wrestling. The University of Iowa accepted him but didn't give him a scholarship.

Campbell paid the tuition with money he earned from odd jobs, then joined the wrestling team as a freshman team walk-on. He stunned the Big Ten by becoming the 177-pound division champion.

"The next year Iowa gave me a full scholarship," said Chris. "I was killing people. Then I tore the ligaments in my right knee near Christmastime."

His aspirations for a national championship that year went out the window with his injury.

A nursing student he met in 1975 and married four years later, Laura Beving, became an inspiration in Campbell's life. He felt she had a lot of gumption to take on the responsibility of making grades and raising a child at the same time.

Having become national champion in 1977 and '78, Campbell set his sights on the Olympics. But he was twice thwarted: In 1980, by the United States boycott of the Games following the Soviet invasion of Afghanistan. The second blow came when he injured his right knee during a workout.

Campbell's frustration over the Olympic boycott was understandable because he had defeated the defending gold medalist. In 1980, he was totally focused on wrestling, coached by Dan Gable, who persuaded Campbell that if he studied and practiced yoga, he would be quicker, more flexible, and experience fewer injuries.

Campbell made the 1980 Olympic Team but didn't compete because of the boycott. To make the team, he practiced yoga every day, ran hard and lifted weights. He said, "I came at competition from a spiritual point of view, and I beat the defending gold medalist fourteen to one, when in other years he had beaten me. I was so upbeat that in the Olympic trials I beat everybody by, I think, at least ten points. I wasn't even breathing heavy and was barely sweating. After wrestling and winning, I'd go and meditate or pray."

The year of the boycott and the injured knee also was for Campbell " the year that proved to me how affecting the great energy source can be when you cultivate it."

"A lot of things happened to me in 1980. There was the boycott, but I won the world championship. I was classified as the most technically prepared wrestler in the world. And when that happened, I reflected on the steps I had taken to get there. I had done Zen meditation; also, counting my breaths really helped my mind to focus, and I did yoga, of course. And then I studied films and wrestled hard and trained hard; and I looked at that process, and I said if I repeat this process in something else I can be successful at anything.

"And so I did that. I wanted to go to law school, and the injured knee which took me out of competition was the impetus. But my grades were really kind of bad — so bad I don't want to say how low they were — but they were so poor I couldn't get into the physical education program at Iowa State University Graduate School."

Campbell put himself into a meditation regimen — the one that was responsible for his fourteen-to-one win over John Peterson. He studied six hours a day for six weeks, heavily involved with meditation and yoga, and then he took the LSAT.

"I scored so high on those exams that I got into a private Ivy League law school — Cornell. I was among the top twenty-five percentile of all people taking the exam. College recruiters started calling me. Before that performance I couldn't have gotten into the dog-catcher's school. So it was illuminating for me to take my spiritual process and see if I could duplicate it. I did that with law school. I never told anybody this story before. My feeling was that people would think I was crazy."

The idea of competitive sport did not take hold of Campbell again until 1989. That was shortly after he began to help coach the Syracuse University team.

There, Campbell said, "I was wrestling with guys three days a week. I found that I was training hard and not getting injured. I was having a real blast. So I started my comeback."

But two blows were to strike Campbell even as he began working to get himself in shape. His mother died of bone cancer in 1991. Then, a few months later, he lost his grandmother to an aneurism. "I hit rock-bottom," said Campbell who experienced, about the same time, his worst loss at the Pan-American games.

Time has helped the wrestler come to peace. Also his spiritual side has given him strength to accept loss.

With the financial support of his employer, Carrier Corporation, Campbell began to travel and compete again. He received a silver medal at the world championships in 1990. But, casting back to the period in his life he thinks was most provocative for him as an athlete who combined mind, body and spirit to excel, was, undeniably, 1980.

What continues to amaze Campbell is the "feeling of total effortlessness I have when I'm spiritually oriented. I think when you meditate you take a lot of stress off of your body. But I was into a very strong spiritual point in 1980, and before then I had never had tournaments where I could wrestle and not feel fatigued at all. Wrestling is a very intense kind of sport. But I was floating, dancing on air in that year. After my match with John Peterson in 1980, after I beat him fourteen to one, I felt like this big light — it was really strange — this big light opened up from the sky and shone down on me and said to me in a voice that only I could hear, 'This is my son and I'm proud of him.' Then I went to a secluded place and prayed. It was funny, I had some friends who were into meditation and practicing alternative lifestyles, and I was walking around after my prayer, and they came up to me and said, 'My God, you're glowing.' I did feel like my aura was particularly strong. I really felt just like I was vibrating a lot. I guess 1980 was my year of peak performance."

If his aura was strong in 1980 to '81, when he earned the title of World Wrestling Champion, it must have been glowing when the thirty-seven-year-old Campbell, whom younger wrestlers affectionately call Grandpa and Old Man, won the Olympic bronze at Barcelona.

The mind, body, spirit enhancement Bob Richards and Chris Campbell define has been demonstrated by rock-climbers who were described by John Macaloon and Mihaly Czikszentmihaly in their book, *Play, Games and Sports in Cultural Context*. The authors related the awesome feeling rock-climbers reported when action, awareness and altered time sense merging in them produced a spiritual lifting, or out-of-body experience. Here is the observation of one rock-climber from their book:

"If you could imagine yourself becoming as clear as when you focus a pair of binoculars; everything's blurred and then the scene becomes clear, as you focus them. If you focus yourself in the same way, until all of you is clear, you don't think of how you are going to do it; you just do it.

"The right decisions are made, but not rationally. Your mind is shut down and your body just goes. It is one of the extremes of human experience."

In the same chapter, the authors observed: "But within this intense concentration, indeed on account of it, there occurs a grand expansion, an opening out to the basic concerns of the human condition, a blossoming invisible to the flatland observer but real and compelling in the minds of the climbers." The authors went on to describe the superlatives used by some climbers to describe their intensified experiences as "transcendent," "religious," "visionary," and "ecstatic."

Macaloon and Czikszentmihaly acknowledged that many of the climbers they studied failed to experience a transcendent feeling when they were stretching themselves, pointing out, "At the present stage of our work it is not yet possible to say anything systematic about why some people report deep-flow experiences, value them absolutely, and pursue them with vigor, while others do not."

Canadian Olympian Kim Alleston spoke of the exalted deep-flow state in these words, as reported by Terry Orlick in *The Pursuit of Excellence:*

"I have experienced flow on several occasions, and to me it was a feeling of separating from my body, from my mind, and letting my body do what came naturally. When this happened, things always went surprisingly well; almost as if my mind would look at what my body was doing and say, 'hey, you're good,' but at the same time not making any judgments on what I was doing because it was not 'me' that was doing it; it was my body. This way, by not making any judgments, it was easy to stay in the present."

We've seen that athletes, and others, can call on body, mind and spirit in concert as demonstrated by Tuck Miller climbing a rugged mountain to save his trapped girlfriend; the tire changer, Charles Dennis Jones, preventing a man from burning to death; Bob Richards winning the gold with a disabling injury; and champion wrestler Chris Campbell, accomplishing far more than an Olympic bronze medal. All of these experiences prove in their own way that every human being has far greater capabilities than he knows, and their extension is available to him, to each of us, to the extent that we learn to bring them into action.

The purpose of this book is to demonstrate methods of achieving superior performance, not only on the track and field, but in the pursuit of champion-like attitudes, behavior and high goals as a commitment to excellence in the whole of life. Marianne Williamson's fierce insight into the human heart, captured in unforgettable words, define exactly the dilemma that hinders all of us from reaching for our best:

"Our deepest fear is not that we are inadequate. Our deepest fear is that we are powerful beyond measure. It is our light, not our darkness, that frightens us."

3

The Magnificent Connection

The universe exists. Perhaps that is a statement which all people accept as truth. If it exists, it was created. That which is created has a creator. That which is created intentionally has a plan, a reason for existence. The universe is not a coincidence, nor is the energy that unites the universe into an orderly system.

Chapter Three asks; "How do we live in harmony with this energy?" How do we align our actions with the intent of universal force? It is this alignment, we believe, that makes the spiritual wind blow to your back, pushing you and carrying you further than you could go swimming against the tide.

When we are doing right — proceeding on the individual course of life that is correct for us — we are assisted by the invisible force. This chapter is about linking up to this energy so that we can be swept to a destiny far greater than what we could achieve operating as a self-contained, isolated entity.

Brian Luke Seaward, sports psychologist, faculty member of New York University, who has coached college and Olympic skaters, as well as members of the Olympic biathlon team, described an intriguing woman when he told us in a telephone interview that Carolyn N. Myss, M.A., an intuitive diagnostician, can look at the aura surrounding a person's body and predict exactly the individual's state of health.

"Not only can she diagnose what ails a person, but she can do it accurately by telephone without ever seeing the person in the flesh," Seaward said.

How does a medical intuitive fit into a chapter devoted in part to explaining resistance to the idea of body-mind-spirit unification? Carolyn Myss fits because her statement in the book, *The Creation of Health,* which she co-authored with C. Norman Shealy, M.D., represents what all of us must accept if we are to embrace the fullness of what it means to be human:

"The time has come to assert one primal fact: the human spirit is real. Beyond the chemical, physical and physiological study of disease, there comes a point, as we search for the cause of illness, when we are led directly to the core of a person's soul. This is a bold notion … it is not, however, original. In recent decades, numerous health professionals have suggested that the cause of illness is ultimately connected to inner stresses present in a person's life.

"The language used to describe this connection between illness and stress varies from source to source. Some use psychological terms, others use the language of stress. Still others emphasize the body-mind-spirit connection. In combining the significance of all this research, it becomes apparent that something of greater value is being universally introduced into our world. Our 'spirits' are longing to be recognized as legitimate, meaning they are every bit as real as our physical selves. Beyond the religious and poetic acceptance of the human spirit, our spiritual natures are breaking through the barriers of the psychological and emotional language, demanding to be identified as the underlying force of life from which all else flows."

Carolyn Myss's statement is unequivocal. She doesn't hint at spirit, or apologize for a viewpoint which is largely anathema to Western medicine and philosophy, a viewpoint which was emphasized in an experience described by author/physician Bernie Siegal, M.D., in the foreword to *The Creation of Health:*

"One of my subversive acts was to post on the bulletin board of the doctors' lounge at Yale-New Haven Hospital a double-blind study of the effectiveness of prayer in avoiding post-myocardial infarction complications. In twenty-four hours someone had written 'bullshit' across it. One cannot change the closed-minded with statistics. Beliefs are matters of faith, not logic. As the Quakers say, 'Speak truth to power.'"

Why are so many of us doubtful, fearful, suspicious — closed minded — to the idea that humans are invigorated by a spiritual reality that encompasses the universe, and is reflected individually in each one of us?

The answer to this fundamental question is so consuming that it has occupied philosophers, men and women of religion and science, mystics, artists, writers, holy leaders, saviors and sages since the time of the stone-age cultures. The xenophobic fanaticism of the great religious crusades, the internecine wars of spiritual domination throughout the ages, the bloody conflicts of expanding empires which drew breath from Holy Reform, all are part of the incorporation of God for the solace of mankind. And all these divergent views are based on different, and often antagonistic, interpretations of the origin of the great spirit, or Godhead.

But persistently, unfailingly, and without regard for the competing religions which have sought domination and authority to speak exclusively for their one supreme God, a coherent body of insight has always prevailed. The central perception of this insight — the Perennial Philosophy — which has existed for more than 5,000 years, is that there is a spiritual reality which is the source of all consciousness. Each of us is joined to this spiritual reality, and in the spiritually evocative expression of sports by its dedicated participants — through the disciplined concentration, the clear hardship of endurance, the stretched limits of physical capacity — there is a significant parallelism with the seekers of unification of mind, body, spirit.

While most of us believe that humans are possessed of a spirit, or soul, we seem to encounter a blind spot when we try to figure out what we should do about it. In sports, as we have said, when an athlete reaches above himself — enters the zone — it is more comfortable to explain his experience as a highly energized state, or demonstration of peak mind/body collaboration — a sort of hypnotic phase brought on by the brain's release of chemicals to produce enhanced power in an excited body. The idea of spirit as the directing force, the mobilizing super-energy that drives the human machine — a dynamic potential as from a battery whose source is the unlimited universe — seems to be too much to swallow.

We get a hint of the magnificent scope of who we are perhaps best from the poets like Swinburne, who wrote:

"I am that which began;
Out of me the years roll;
Out of me God and man;
I am equal and whole;
God changes, and man,
And the form of them bodily.
I am the soul."

But it is Carolyn Myss who presents most clearly the argument of the dogged pragmatists who view humans as creatures of the earth fearful of a spiritual brightness they will not acknowledge because it cannot be measured: "... the existence of a God, or of any invisible divine force, cannot be proven to the satisfaction of the scientific or agnostic mind. The type of 'proof' available — miracles, healings, apparitions, personal faith and other phenomena of that nature — means nothing to those who seek something more tangible or repeatable in terms of scientific methodology.

"There is, however, one attribute of the human being that is seemingly acknowledged across the many lines of thinking about such matters, and that is the existence of the human 'spirit' — whether accepted poetically or literally.

"When the spirit of someone is not present, the creation or physical matter that belongs to that person disintegrates. We all know the expressions, 'to break one's spirit' or 'team spirit' or a 'nation's spirit.' These are references to the power and reality of the human spirit.

"Anyone who has witnessed the gradual lessening of someone's spirit [or enthusiasm] for life, for a relationship, or for his or her work knows what it is to see the physical part of that person's life shrivel into dust. Without the participation of the human spirit, nothing can remain in healthy physical form.

"This is absolutely real in the world of healing. Those who heal have spirit. Spirit is essential to the healing process, and when any individual is unable to engage the power of his or her own spirit on the healing journey, that person is preparing to die."

"Spiritual development," Myss says, "is the process of giving attention to the deeper capacities and qualities of human nature and working to perfect them. The discipline of non-attachment, for example, is the practice of becoming so personally empowered that you are able to interact in every situation in your life, contributing the highest degree of insight and wisdom, without needing to control the outcome of events."

In a very real sense, non-attachment was the condition in which Tuck Miller fought his way up the mountain when he shouldn't have been able to. And non-attachment, the sense of controlling the outcome of events without apparent effort to do so, is one of the common signs that athletes describe as peculiar to the zone.

It is the whole concept of releasing control — giving into the spiritual power of our nature — that frightens us. Sports psychologist Brian Luke Seaward describes the process by which we diminish the potential of spirit by obfuscating its purpose:

"The point is, it doesn't matter what we call it — the divine force, the non-local God, the Magnificent Connection, whatever — the minute we label it, we weigh it down with all the baggage of what we've been taught. And since we've got an emotional investment in what we've been taught, we defend our interpretation of the divine force and often condemn other interpretations as wrong, blasphemous, unsacred, or dangerous.

"The fact is, we can't articulate it in words. It's something we know intuitively — but we keep trying to defend it because we want so much to believe in the brightness we sense dwells in us. We sense it but distrust it because it overwhelms us. It frightens us because we think to submit to it means giving away control of ourselves, as if precise management of the universe of self is the only method by which we establish out identity on earth.

"Often, the divine energy is compromised when the ego or left brain steps in and says, 'I'm in charge here. I won't stand for anything to challenge my authority.'

"When people enter the zone — and they certainly don't have to be athletes to do it — they have released ego, they've leaped past the boundaries of the universe of self, and have become one with the force — with unlimited energy."

Because the nature of the divine force, The Magnificent Connection, the non-local God, is so controversial for many in sports, as well as in other endeavors, we asked Brian Luke Seaward if an athlete or any person who enters the zone can benefit from the power of the association, yet be unaware, or even doubtful, of the identity, magnitude and source of the power.

His reply was that the source of power has been described as an endless river without any fences or boundaries of time into which any person, regardless of his beliefs or persuasions, may reach to furnish his spirit with light and energy.

His analogy sparked a less-lofty reminder in us of a scene played in a popular movie of the 1960s in which actors Cary Grant and Sophia Loren starred.

In the movie *Houseboat,* Grant, the recently widowed father of a boy and girl, is trying to explain to his nine-year-old son, still troubled with the death of his mother, that death is not the end of life.

Father and son are sitting on the floor of the houseboat with their feet dangling over the water. Grant picks up an empty bottle and dips it into the water, holds it up to the light and says, "Think of my body as this bottle. What happens to it when I die?"

He pours the water from the bottle into the lake.

"See," he says, "it doesn't disappear, it doesn't die. It becomes part of something bigger."

Spiritual understanding for Peter Westbrook — 1984 Olympic bronze medal winner in the saber, six-time Olympic competitor — came about indirectly as inspiration from his mother, he said. A determined Japanese woman, descended from a line of Samurai warriors, who married a black American, she gave her fourteen-year-old son Peter, who was in and out of trouble, five dollars on the condition that he spend it on a fencing lesson.

"My mother saw that if I got involved in a sport like basketball many of the people I would be mixing with would be the same as the environment I was already in," he said.

"In her mind, this was a no-win situation," he explained, adding: "Later, she told me she was certain that if I got into fencing, I would meet people like doctors and lawyers, a big cut above the kind of people I'd probably meet if I had gotten into boxing or karate."

Westbrook, described by a *Newark Star Ledger* writer as a person "... who possesses, for example, the tempera- ment of El Cordobes, the famous matador; the agility of Julius Erving, the basketball great; the cunning of Muhammed Ali, the legend of boxing; the gracefulness of Rudolph Nureyev, ballet's living shrine ..." has been the national saber fencing champion for an unprecedented thirteen times. Even more remarkable, after winning his first national championship in 1974, Westbrook was saber champion for eight consecutive years.

Westbrook credits fencing as responsible for everything he has achieved in his life, becoming America's most accomplished fencer in generations, and the head of the Peter Westbrook Foundation, a vehicle to introduce disadvantaged youths to fencing through weekly clinics at the New York Fencers Club.

With a gift from himself of several thousand dollars to the foundation, he began to help others and put together a board of directors which included the late tennis great, Arthur Ashe; the famed Wilma Rudolph; and John Brandemas, the former president of New York University.

Westbrook's idea was that if fencing could rescue him from the low-income housing projects of Newark, the drug dealers, the fighting and the aimlessness, why couldn't it do the same for other youngsters?

Fencing was a catalyst for his scholarship to New York University, from which he graduated in 1975. He then worked eleven years as a marketing representative for North American Van Lines and traveled the world as an athlete.

Westbrook's own experience with the zone is best exemplified by his description of a competition between himself and a rude, arrogant Cuban fencing champion who was matched against the American. At stake was the 1995 Pan-American Games championship.

Westbrook said the Cuban was a towering six-foot-three-inch black man who looked down at Westbrook, a sturdy five-foot-nine inches, with contempt, and said in street language, "I'm going to ---- you, man."

Westbrook knew the Cuban was bent on demoralizing him, reducing his confidence, convincing him that he was foolish to imagine that he could win against such a superior competitor. The man succeeded in intimidating him.

"You know, boxers sometimes try to stare you down to convince you that they're really going to tear you apart, and they act as though they really feel that way. Well, this guy had me feeling that way too. When I practiced with him, maybe four days later, he looked at me disdainfully, checked me out, and the coach said to me, 'Practice with him.'

"I said, sure, and he kicked my ass. He wasn't really even trying. I can tell when somebody is trying his best. I was trying with eighty, maybe ninety percent of me, and he was trying with maybe sixty percent of himself.

"I said to myself, 'Damn, I've got a big problem. The only way I can beat this guy, and I know I can, is if I'm in the zone and the spirit touches me. I know I can do it then.'

"Those kinds of things you can't really call at will, you really can't command your body, mind and spirit to be in unison. When it happens, it's almost like a gift. I've tried many times. I say I'm going to call on my mind, body, spirit and discover, hey, I'm far from it, nothing there. Hello? Hello? No answer. Hello? Hello? No answer."

"This time," Westbrook said, he told himself the zone was the only way. "My body was in great shape because of lifting weights. My mind was in good shape, and the mind is something you have to work on because it can play tricks on you. It can raise all sorts of fears — fear that you can't do it, fear that you're not ready, fear that the opponent is so great, fear of your emotions, fear of how you will feel one minute from now."

There is no room for fear in the zone, however. Westbrook said that when, through meditation or prayer, he enters the quiet space of the zone, he can feel his sword hand is almost like a magic wand, literally like a magic wand.

"When I have this magic in my hand, it's like the power that can turn a lion into a mouse. I can do almost anything then, and it works."

Apparently the power worked when Westbrook next fenced with the Cuban. It happened at the Gold Medal match when the man reminded the American of what he was going to do to him with the same nasty insult he had used on Westbrook previously.

Westbrook responded by thinking, "My body is in great shape and my mind is firm. So I went again to the spirit, not just to overcome the threat of the Cuban, but to be granted the wisdom and sharpness to win. I have to admit," Westbrook said, "I wanted to win this time because this guy had humiliated me; his spirit was not clean, a little bit contaminated. I could feel his contamination, I could feel his arrogance, his ego. I'd been that way myself many times before I learned about the spirit. I wasn't that way then; I had meditated and prayed for two days to get into the zone so that I could teach the Cuban a lesson. I needed to be in the zone to do that. I needed the magic wand."

"What happened was remarkable," Westbrook said. Throughout the match, as the sabers flashed, pointed, touched steel, parried and thrust, the American floated as if in a dream. He could do nothing wrong. No step in his smooth dance, his ballet of swordplay, was taken wrong.

Westbrook explained that a normal win of eleven points out of a possible fifteen would be judged as excellent. He vanquished his opponent fifteen to five. It was a total rout. The American described the scene in this fashion:

"… I felt an electric shock run through the crowd. They seemed to understand what was happening. I think in that brief instant we fused, the crowd and I. Reality, as I knew it, no longer existed and time became suspended. We opened the gateway to another world and passed through. The man was crying, snuffling, tears on his cheeks. The crowd knew the magic, and I could feel the electricity in the magic of the moment. It was something … beyond reality."

Westbrook's experience with the Cuban was more real, he said, than everyday existence. It was something beyond reality.

The fencer said that after the match was concluded he had to drop down on his knees and say thanks. Then he got up and told his opponent, "Don't feel that bad, buddy, don't worry about it. The man was crying, and I slapped him on the back. That's all I could say to him. He had no idea about the enormous power of the miraculous force centered in me that won the match."

Westbrook's positive nature, his gentleness, his path to the zone, he credits to his mother, a woman who loved to live in Newark, a big city full of threats and danger. His faith in God was the solace he leaned on when Mariko Westbrook was killed in a tragic 1994 attack Newarkers still remember. As an account of her death in the *New York Times* reported, "One of the saddest parts of the story is that Mrs. Westbrook, pummeled for giving the wrong person a bit of neighborly advice, was murdered after her worries were over.

"She had endured a lot. Against the wishes of her wealthy family in Japan, she married an American serviceman who, in turn, left her with two babies. Then she ignored her family's advice to return home alone, setting out to make a life for her baby son and daughter in Newark.

"It worked our beautifully. Her daughter, Vivian, grew up to become an insurance executive. Her son, Peter, became a marketing executive and the first American fencer in twenty-four years to win an Olympic medal [bronze, Los Angeles, 1984].

"Peter Westbrook, a gentle man with his mother's features, said he and his sister used to ask her, 'Mom, wouldn't you like to move?' She'd say, 'No, I like it here.'

"Mrs. Westbrook had become a Newarker. She raised her two children in Hayes Homes when the housing project was a real community. After retiring she kept her friends at her assembly-line job at a picture-tube manufacturer.

"Neighbors admired the way she raised her children. She put them through twelve years of Catholic school, working off the tuition cleaning the church and helping out on Bingo nights. She bribed Peter into taking fencing lessons at a local school when he was thirteen, giving him $5 each day he went to class, until he was hooked."

According to the *Times,* Mariko Westbrook's favorite thing was going to Newark's Penn Station to feed the homeless people. People who knew her, even the drug addicts, used to watch over her.

Mrs. Westbrook was attacked on December 29 by a surly 200-pound young woman after she got on a bus following a shopping trip for half-price Christmas ribbons and wrapping paper at Woolworth's.

The attacker started viciously pummeling Mrs. Westbrook after the latter was heard by bus riders to give the woman kindly advice about loosening the scarves wrapping the woman's baby. Infuriated, the woman struck Mariko Westbrook repeatedly in the face, despite horrified protests from bus riders. One elderly man who tried to stop the murderous raining of blows was thrown off the woman's back.

As Mrs. Westbrook rushed out of the stopped bus, she was kicked by the woman, sending her flying to crash on the hard, cold cement headfirst. She died four days later.

Peter Westbrook, the champion fencer, the man of humanity who works with impoverished kids to give them the encouragement and hope he received from his mother, remembers the most important woman in his life for the phone calls she made to him from her apartment in the heart of Newark: "Oh, Peter, I so happy."

Peter Westbrook, like Chris Campbell, Bob Richards, and hundreds of other enlightened athletes, discovered that both sport and the spiritual state grow out of a demanding urge to express the richness of life. In both adventures, there are a variety of ways to practice the process of self-exceeding.

Lanny Bassham, the 1976 Olympic gold medal rifle marksman, proved to be an eloquent exponent of the exploration into the potential of human possibility. In Bassham's case, his confidence in himself soared and led him to the gold in Montreal in 1976, after winning the second-place silver in Munich in 1972.

For an Olympic athlete to say that the best thing that ever happened to him was not capturing a gold medal the first time out may sound strange. For Bassham, that statement reflected an honest self-appraisal following interviews he pursued with other champions.

Hours of practice and hard work earned Bassham a spot on the 1972 United States Olympic rifle team, pitting him against the world's best in Munich. His effort was not quite good enough and he had to settle for a silver medal.

"I choked terribly in 1972," he said. "I worked very hard, but I wasn't prepared mentally."

For the next four years, Bassham talked to Olympic winners to find out why they won. What made them special? He discovered the answer was mental preparedness that separated champions from "the athletes who just played."

Bassham put this information to work and designed his own method for mental management. The results paid off: world championships in both 1974 and 1978, and an Olympic gold medal in 1976. Now he teaches athletes and non-athletes alike how to reach their goals by practicing mental management. His book, *With Winning in Mind,* has sold more than 100,000 copies.

A former United States Army rifle expert, Bassham demonstrated the real spirit of sports during the 1976 Olympics when he and his fellow Olympic team member, Margaret Murdock, both chalked up equal totals of 1,162 points to finish the small-bore fifty-meter shooting event in a tie. Under Olympic rules, a tie is broken by determining the best shooter in the last ten shots of the final round of competition. Bassham, who objected to what he considered the unfairness of the tie-breaking procedure, was awarded the victory. At the awards ceremony, Bassham surprised millions of viewers around the world and Olympic officials by forthrightly pulling Murdock up to the top platform so that she, too, could share in the moment that every Olympic athlete dreams of: the playing of his country's national anthem. It was the first time a winning athlete had ever so honored another competitor at an awards ceremony.

Bassham believes that people do not get what they want unless they are willing to change, unless they match their aspirations with determination, hard work and application.

"It's like making steel," he said. "You put it in a fire, heat it up, and see what happens. Some of the steel will break. Some of it will get stronger."

The credit for his own personal strengthening, Bassham feels, is his recognition of how the conscious and subconscious work to produce, for him, a model of performance.

That model is built around a belief that the conscious mind is incapable of high levels of performance, Bassham said. "It is the great limiter of human performance. If we could bypass the negativity and limitations of the conscious mind, we could unlock huge abilities, physical and otherwise, in individuals. I have no doubt that the power of the subconscious mind is hard to even approach. It's like thinking how big the universe is. If we keep going out from the earth, where does it end? I think the capacity of the human being is unlimited, and I believe it's unlimited because we are born without any limitations. This unlimited ability we have is in the image of God; it's what we have in common with God, and we hardly use any of it."

We asked Lanny Bassham if he meant that spirit and unconscious mind are synonymous.

He replied:

"I'm saying the spirit is composed of what I call a triad — the conscious, subconscious and self-image — all are spiritual. Not just one — all are spiritual. I'll show you why. The self-image is that part of your mind that makes you act like you. It's your habits, your attitudes, your behavioral style. It's what makes you you. Your self-image and your performance are forever linked. If I think I can beat you, and you think I can beat you, it's a done deal.

"Now let me interject God into the conscious mind. Together a task that may have been daunting to you alone becomes easier because you have a connection to the Creator, to the Power. Our self-image is changed to a winning perspective because God doesn't fail. Never! Now you say to yourself, 'My self-image is to win. It's like me to win. I deserve to win.'

"When the conscious mind, the subconscious mind and the self-image are all balanced and working together, good performance is easy. And all this can be done without God. Yes, I know it sounds contradictory, but it isn't. I know athletes who never think about God, but their conscious feeling is, 'I can do it.' The subconscious says to them, 'I went out and trained, and I got my body in shape.' And their self-image says, 'I did this and it's like me to win.' And they win."

We asked Lanny Bassham another question: "In other words, you're saying that a lot of athletes who get into the zone experience it as an out-of-their-normal body performance range, not in a spiritual sense at all?"

Bassham said, "Yes, that's true, as far as it goes. An atheist can tap into the spirit without any belief in God. Think of God, the spirit, like sunshine. It's there for everybody to share. So, if you can tap into good and never connect it to God, you accomplish in the same way. You can say, 'This is a beautiful day; that's just the way it is.' I might say, 'Isn't this a beautiful day God has made?' Either way of saying it, of acknowledging the beauty, doesn't change the fact that God made the day. It's just that many of us don't recognize that He did it."

Bassham made an important point about how a person interprets the power that comes from spirit:

"If we think the power comes from us as opposed to something else, then it has a much greater chance of corrupting a person's life than it does of enriching it. If we have the vision to see that God, with all the power, is there like a silent battery that we can plug into, then that's the beginning of wisdom. God is there whether you recognize Him or not. And God loves you whether you want to love Him or not. That's my biased view as a New Testament Christian, and everything I do is filtered through this understanding."

Bassham pointed out that when he started coaching it was with the understanding that he was helping another person with his dream, and that coaching was part of his responsibility, his individual journey to maturity. Passing on the joy so that it can start a spark in another person is a responsibility of the enlightened individual, Bassham said. He expressed this attitude when he observed, "If you take your hand and put it in the hand of another, your dream will live forever. That's the ultimate connection to God. It's what the Beatles meant when they sang, 'The love you take is equal to the love you make.'"

Passing on the joy so that it can be a spark of joy to another — far from being exclusive with Lanny Bassham, the gold-medal Olympian who happens to be a Christian — is one message that coaches all over America are taking up on the playing field. Hundreds of college coaches and thousands in high school are carrying out an organized crusade with the help of more than a hundred evangelical sports ministries.

As an article in *The Oregonian* put it, "The Bible is their play book. A macho Jesus is their inspiration."

Coaches who crusade for Jesus on the playing fields are merely expressing the spirit in their fashion, but as Lanny Bassham would say, "It doesn't matter what the nature of your spiritual belief is, or whether you have one at all. What does matter, if the individual is going to achieve a life of accomplishment and high personal excellence, is to accept that there is a power which — in sports endeavors and in other physical and mental activities — makes itself known by responding to the passion of the individual."

Conversely, as dozens of sports psychologists have observed, negativity in the individual — often characterized as a lack of spiritual conviction — can interfere with a person's ability to accomplish what he or she was born to do.

Identical twins Sarah and Karen Josephson, gold and silver Olympic medalists in synchronized swimming, are not in doubt about the zone as a state of excellence which they have entered in the grueling sport of competition swimming. The Josephsons are both five-feet-four-inches and 120 pounds and have been swimming together for twenty years. Being identical twins is a distinct advantage in a sport that demands perfection and rewards mirror-image synchronization. Twins also have another advantage. "I think we can read each other's minds sometimes," said Sarah. No strangers to high-level competition, the Josephsons' synchronized swim team swam away with a silver medal in the 1988 Olympics and a gold in 1992.

Sarah Josephson told us that, "By the time Karen and I graduated from high school, we were probably ranked about number five or six in synchronized swimming in the country. I went to Ohio State, and they have a varsity synchronized swimming team. Karen and I competed collegiately and in United States nationals, but our first international competition was in 1980. In 1984 we tried out as a duet, and we got second place in the Olympic trials."

The rest, as they say, is history.

Sarah said her experiences in the zone could be described as equivalent to spiritual ecstasy. "When it first started happening," she said," I was in the senior competition. I experienced the zone in short periods of time, like thirty seconds up to two minutes, and, for me, it was like everything seemed to flow, as if you didn't really have to think about what was coming next or what to do. It just happened, and I knew that it was going to go right. It definitely happened in 1992 at the Olympics in our final swim. Well, actually, in both of them. The prelims and final swim. Karen and I were in the zone for most of the time. We talked about it. I was aware of it because there were specific times where I seemed to come back into myself for a few seconds, and I said to myself, 'Wow, this is the Olympics, and you know we're here and this is it,' and then everything kind of went back into the groove again and it was very easy and I was not really thinking. It just happened without really having to think about what was going on."

Sarah said there have been a few other times in her life, when she was running hard or biking, when she was able to enter the fluid, zone state.

Sarah admitted feeling reluctant to imply that there's a spiritual dimension to the zone "because some people get uncomfortable with that," she said.

Sarah said Duke Zelinski, the coach who trained her and her sister, was able to show both women a procedure for entering the zone to increase performance.

A different concept of the zone comes from Joan Ullyot, who considers those who enter into the elevated sphere of the spiritual as blessed. Presently a world-ranked masters (over forty) distance runner, Dr. Joan L. Ullyot is best known as an authority on sports medicine and psychology, with an emphasis on women's athletic/health concerns.

A graduate of Wellesley College and Harvard Medical School, she has done research in cellular pathology, the psychology of high achievement, exercise physiology and preventive medicine. She also has an active private practice in sports psychology and psychotherapy, with a Jungian orientation. This former self-described "creampuff" took up running in 1971, at age thirty, and quickly evolved into one of America's top women distance runners. She was a member of the United States national marathon team from 1974 to 1979, was third in the national championships in 1975 and 1976, and, since age forty, has won numerous medals in the World Veterans Marathon, and in 1988, at age forty-eight, she ran a personal-best time of 2:47:39 for the 26.2-mile marathon, almost four minutes faster than her previous best set at age thirty-six.

Ullyot responded to questions in our interview of her on the subject of the zone, and The Magnificent Connection, with some refreshing thoughts:

"I went for a run after our talk," she said, "and, of course, thought of all kinds of things I should have mentioned but didn't! Chief among these was my response to the question about whether one could learn to tap into this force, or flow, or source of energy, that we were discussing. I find myself vaguely uneasy about the concept of learning to use this power because, in my experience, it finds us and uses us, rather than vice-versa. To be touched by it is like an act of grace by something above (or beyond) us; to think of harnessing this power for our own ends smacks of hubris, if not sacrilege.

"So what can the aspiring athlete, or monk, or warrior do? How can one excel and remain ego-less to the degree required? To my mind, what we have to learn to do is pay attention to the subtle manifestations of this force, and thus honor it. This attention includes being aware of what is going on in our bodies (breathing, muscular movements, pain, whatever) as well as in the world around us. It means not forcing our own will upon these things, but moving with them. Discipline, yes, but not rigidity. In terms of running, this would translate, for instance, into running the workout that your body is ready and happy to do, not just the one that your schedule (or someone else's that you've borrowed) calls for! In other words, being mindful of your body as an equal partner in this endeavor, not just a slave to your ego goals.

"In some ways I see modern technology, e.g., the heart-rate monitor, as interfering with this process of self-knowledge. I have seen many people who exercise according to the numbers on their readout and don't have a clue as to how they actually are feeling, how their lungs and legs are doing — which is what should determine the workout. The technology can further sever mind from body, which I believe is one of the primary problems in our civilization. Thomas Moore refers to this lack of attention as "loss of soul."

Ulloyot said that she knew for certain that strange, remarkable experiences like the mountain-climbing epic of Tuck Miller, or the strength of tire changer Charles Dennis Jones rescuing a truck driver from a smashed-in cab, were indeed true. One such experience happened to her. The occasion was an automobile accident on the Oakland Bay Bridge in 1974, when Ulloyot's automobile was overturned in an accident. With what was later diagnosed as a fractured skull and broken collarbone, Ulloyot nevertheless, with single-minded determination, lifted the vehicle off of a friend who had been thrown from the passenger seat and trapped underneath the car.

On another occasion, Ulloyot was running in San Francisco's Presidio area with her younger son, John, and her dog on a leash. She had heard about a pack of wild dogs roaming in the area, but never expected to encounter them.

The pack found the lone woman, her son and dog, and swarmed to attack. Ulloyot's own dog ran behind her and cowered, but the master runner faced the snarling animals and, wielding her dog's chain leash, shouted at them, "If you come at us, I will kill you."

There was no doubt in Ulloyot's mind that she would kill every one of the dogs with her bare hands and the chain. Her fierce message convinced the animals, and they turned tail and ran away.

"Those dogs recognized the total conviction in me, and it frightened them. They ran for their lives."

We asked Joan if, with the kind of total confidence she demonstrated, can athletes, can anybody, reach into themselves and find the zone?

She said, "My experience has been that top athletes, when they have mastered their sport, tap into it because that's one reason they are champions — they have that focus, or they can get that focus. The whole purpose of the sports psychology field, which I've been involved with for fifteen years, is to take this thing that some people have as a natural gift at and teach it. However, I don't think it's ever as good taught as it is when it happens naturally. And I think in a way that's what distinguishes champions from others."

We asked Joan Ulloyot another question. "You are saying that, by getting into the zone, getting in harmony with the force of the universe, one can increase one's own force?"

Ulloyot said, "Yeah, it works. I've experienced it. That's why I'm a Jungian. He (Jung) felt the same way. There's definitely a force — I call it the source, and I've had a kind of mystical experience. One so deep I don't want to talk about it. It occurred one night in my bedroom, and it was such an awesome experience that I will forever be inspired and transformed by it. The thing about when you have such an experience is that you can't do it all the time. It happens on very, very rare occasions. It would be over-powering otherwise. It is overpowering. but you always know that it's there. Afterwards, the experience gives you a kind of faith; you know it as the source of your own being."

Ulloyot pointed out that the psychologist Jung observed that we all think that we're separate people, indi-viduals, but in fact we're just like little islands, and down at sea level everybody is tapped into this one organism." I think what happens when we enter the zone is that we get to this sea level; we're tapping into the vast experience — not just of human beings but of this other source beyond," Ulloyot said.

She told us an experience she had while running with a friend of hers, Michael Murphy, one of the authors of *The Zone: The Psychic Side of Sports.*

"Let me just tell you a little story. I was running with Michael Murphy way back in the seventies, and I was actually the person who got him to run long and run his first marathon because he would always give out in fifteen to twenty miles. I remember saying to Michael, 'You're running too fast; run with me, at my pace, and we'll get you there,' and so we did.

"Anyway, he was talking about this book he was writing, on the psychic side of sports, and he asked my opinion as a very practically oriented doctor. I was studying sports medicine at the time, I guess. Anyway, he said, 'You know there are all kinds of psychic phenomena that happen to people in sports; probably you have experienced this yourself.'

"And I said, 'No, actually I haven't experienced any psychic phenomena of any kind as far as I know, and I've been running about eight years. Can you give me an example of what you mean?'

"He said, 'Yes, for instance, time is always distorted; sometimes it goes very fast, sometimes very slowly, and don't you ever wake up and realize that you're miles or hours further on?'

"I said, 'Oh, yeah, but that happens every time I run, that's just normal running.'

"'That's what you thought was normal running?' he asked.

"I replied, 'Yes. I thought that was normal running and, in fact, there is this tremendous distortion that goes on when you get into anything like that.'

"'You didn't realize you were in what we call the 'zone'?'

"Exactly."

Sarah Josephson and Dr. Joan Ullyot confirm, as hundreds of athletes have, that the zone, The Magnificent Connection, is the experience which creates a stronger reality by which we can derive a clearer definition of who we are. It is an exciting prospect!

Medical intuitive Carolyn Myss put this idea very clearly in her book, *Creating Health,* when she wrote:

"We create our own reality. The tools that we use to engage the process of creation are all invisible. They are our attitudes, beliefs, values, ethics and emotional energies. Negative attitudes about life diminish the life-force itself. Like damming up a river, negativity on this scale is equal to continually disregarding the value and purpose of one's own life. The life-force gradually, but continually, becomes weakened. The body, the mind and the spirit begin to suffer from 'energy malnutrition.' If this downward spiral continues unchecked, the spirit experiences energy starvation. Eventually, it becomes impossible to replenish the spirit, and the body consequently dies.

"The process of creation continues during downward spirals. So long as we have breath, we have the power to create. What is created is always a reflection of the energy present in a person's system. When downward cycles are created, depression results. A person's life-force becomes literally depressed and void of vitality. The body begins to feel like lead, and exhaustion becomes a person's constant companion. This is one example of what spiritual starvation feels like.

"Because of our orientation toward physical matter, the idea of life force may not be easily appreciated as having validity, much less as having power to it. Yet it exists. During an intuitive health evaluation, the strength of an individual's life-force is my indicator as to how committed that person is to remaining alive."

Since the way of champions is one avenue to make a connection with the spirit, it seems useful to conclude this chapter with an experiment which may help to change your life:

Life is a day-by-day experiment. We try new behaviors and evaluate them to determine if they add or detract from the life that we desire. The willingness to experiment, to try new ways, to display different dimensions of ourselves, is the choice to grow.

A thirty-day experiment in living is a small investment as a means to discover a more rewarding life. The thirty-day experiment described below could alter your life beyond anything you have imagined. Winning the lottery is tiny in comparison.

For thirty days, live as if an external force was assisting you in everything you do. Act as if this energy was around you constantly, and your every action drew from or contributed to it. When you are awake, say to yourself, "I feel a great energy source around me. As you drive to work, look at the flowers and trees and sense that everything living is wishing you well, sending you silent thoughts of well-being. Wink at a big tree to acknowledge the energy exchange between you (it is the tree that gives you oxygen for free because that is its purpose). At a red light, be thankful that you are stopped to give other drivers a chance to get to their destinations. Feel the warmth of the sun. Listen to the wind; taste its freshness.

Seek, with all your senses — especially your intuition — a feeling of connectedness with everything about you. Feel extra energy and say to yourself that this energy is the Good Will of the universe. Act as if your spiritual component is paving the way for success. Don't doubt; doubting will erode from the objectiveness of the experiment. At the end of every day, ask yourself, "Was my life better today because of my new outlook? Do I feel like I am collecting energy and having more to give away to others toward the tasks of the day?"

4

Discovering Who You Are

━━━ ▪ ━━━ ▪ ━━━ ▪ ━━━ ▪ ━━━ ▪ ━━━ ▪ ━━━

It is unfortunate, and totally unnecessary, that so many people in our Western society feel lost, confused about their desires in life, and unsure about careers, commitments, interests, values, and lifestyles. This confusion is a quagmire that slowly swallows human potential. Although entire books are devoted to the lifelong obligation of self-discovery, we believe the quickly-applied tools in this chapter can serve as a foundation for discovering the self.

Answering the question, "Who am I?" is a prerequisite for discovering "Where am I going?" and "How will I get there?" The more we search within ourselves, the more convinced we will become that we possess eternity in our souls.

As we have said, the prerequisite to answering the weighty question of "Who am I?" lies in defining your values, then drawing your life-map. The important issues of life become sorted and clear when you do these things. Lost energy will be retrieved and applied to the outcomes you desire.

If you haven't written what your key values in life mean to you, then your life-map is a blank page. As an important exercise, for the next five days, write a description (similar to the example in this chapter) of one or two personal values. As you write your values, you will be filling in the map that shows the routes you will travel to reach your life's destination. Make a copy of your values and reduce it to fit as the first page of your daily organizer. Review your values frequently, and be sure that everything written into your organizer brings you value.

Building a life-map is the first important step toward describing your major purpose. When you discover what that is, you will be amazed at how the energy of the universe seems to come to you to give you power to achieve it.

We ended Chapter Three with an experiment the reader might wish to take on to expose himself to the power of the universe. It is a step toward human enfoldment. Human enfoldment also is observed in the discipline required of athletes to excel, to improve their bodies. Such effort is similar to the intense concentration (centering, meditation) required of those who seek to stretch their spiritual understanding as they search for higher and higher levels of enlightenment. We believe that — even in the midst of turmoil and violence in our society, a culture which on the surface seems to be embracing drugs, crudity, and immorality — there is strong and growing evidence of many people stretching themselves to the limits of their physical, mental and spiritual capacities. People urgently seek the spiritually evocative, the experiences that can lift them to a spiritual reality, which is the source of all consciousness.

Rock climber Rob Schultheis, described in his book, *Bone Games,* a "spiritual reality," an experience with the Source of All Consciousness during a descent on Mount Neva:

"...the only way down was a pillar of black water ice; I shinnied down it, hands jammed between the ice and the rock face, boot heels jammed against the mountain, toes against the tissue-thin ripples in the great icicle's flank. Impossible, absurd. Then a vertical pitch of rock, nothing to hold on to and fifteen feet of it, and I clung to the grain of the granite — no, but I did — and moved down over it, onto more ice-scoured ledges."

He added: "Looking back on it, I really cannot explain or describe properly that strange person I found inhabiting my body that afternoon. It was just too different from my everyday self, and I have never seen its like before, nor have I seen it since, except for a split second in Mexico in 1982, and a few strange weeks of long-distance running....The person I became on Neva was the best possible version of myself, the person I should have been throughout my life. No regrets, no hesitation; there were no false moves left in me. I really believe I could have hit a mosquito in the eye with a pine needle at thirty paces; I couldn't miss because there was no such thing as a miss. It didn't matter whether I fell or not, because I could not fall, any more than two plus two can equal three. It was all sublime nonsense, of course, but I believed it, down in my very cells; if I hadn't believed, I would have been hurled into the Pit below ... Joy filled me, from the soles of my feet to the tips of the hairs on my head."

For the person who has not experienced "an opening of himself" — the type we have described many times in this book — such transformative experiences as the one described by Schultheis may seem farfetched, if not unbelievable. Yet cynicism cannot dismiss the insistent sense of doubt that may assail the questioning individual. To which Schultheis made an answer when he concluded that humans lost a vital part of themselves when they let go of the "intuitive and powerful world" that comes to people who practice high-risk sports or those who have been awakened by a spiritual conversion.

And that "intuitive and powerful part" which helps define the person is what this chapter is all about. Discovering who you are is both a journey and a process through various stages. Where you begin the journey will depend on your own self-assessment. There are tools which we present in this and the next chapter to make a self-assessment, to help you arrive at the answer of who you are. And inevitably, the reader who perseveres in the search for self-discovery will learn that his journey never ends: it merely takes him from one stage to the next higher one, where at some level he embraces the poignant wisdom that there is an interior grace, a Magnificent Connection, that transcends the world's seemingly unguided events.

So now, please accept the fact that whatever your present status, you are involved in one stage or another on the path to wisdom. Whether you're intent upon losing weight, finding a better job, lowering your golf score, controlling your temper, seeking peace with your past, or taking the first tentative step toward spiritual enlightenment, you must fully engage your willpower, imagination, emotions and intellect to get results. But whatever your goal, you will be able to accomplish it more satisfactorily if you start with a clearer understanding of who you are at the beginning.

One stage in the path of his own self-discovery was experienced by one of the authors, four-time Olympian Lyle Nelson. Nelson was approached by the national team coach for the biathlon event at the 1980 Winter Olympics in Lake Placid, New York.

Art Stegen came up to Nelson as he was removing his skis following his ten-kilometer sprint in a field of about sixty contenders.

"Well, Lyle," he said, "what did you think of your race?"

"Oh, not good, not bad, mediocre, I guess."

"How did you expect to place?" Stegen asked. "You came in number nineteen."

Nelson looked at his coach with surprise. He couldn't give the man an honest answer, and he realized that Stegen knew he had not focused on winning. Later, alone in his room at the dormitory for Olympic athletes, Nelson reflected that during the four years he had worked hard to prepare himself for competition his entire focus had been on "showing up" — honing his abilities so that he could be included among the favored few from around the world who were selected to compete at the zenith of sports events. But showing up was not enough, he realized; he had failed to create an image of himself as an Olympic winner, a champion among champions.

The revelation was startling to him because it meant that he had not pictured himself as a winner, but as a participant. True, his focus on becoming an Olympian had been above average; he had fulfilled his dream, but it fell short of the purpose of the Olympics: to do your personal best in your chosen sport. In this respect he had failed. But far more subtle to Nelson in his disappointment with himself was the inescapable conclusion that he had foreshortened his achievements as an Olympian by not defining them, by not defining himself.

Slowly, it came to him with deep clarity and a little sinking feeling that he did not know what Lyle Nelson stood for. That was a troubling discovery which was to pop up in his mind for the remaining days of the 1980 Winter Olympics, and for years after. He came to a solution much later when it dawned on him that his duty, his quest, his responsibility in life, was to create himself as a new idea, which was constantly changing, growing and merging with a future more perfect self. There would never be a finished person in Lyle Nelson, but there would be completed stages in his development. Each stage of growth would call upon him to re-establish the moral definition of who he was — the basis, enlarged and improved, with each advancing step of body, mind and spirit.

Nelson began more seriously studying the athletic champions with whom he had been associated to discover how they defined themselves and the singlemindedness with which they addressed the idea of winning. Twelve years after his self-scrutiny at Lake Placid, Nelson had talked to hundreds of athletes and successful men and women in every aspect of business, social and sports life. Out of his observations came a deep understanding of the process of self-discovery which inevitably leads the individual to a better conception of himself, accompanied by an ability to set and accomplish far-reaching goals.

Typical of the men and women Nelson and co-author Thorn Bacon have interviewed, people who have developed a clear definition of themselves as absolutely necessary to the success they achieved, is Marty Liquori.

Liquori is one of only three high schoolers to have broken the four-minute mile, and at age eighteen he was among the youngest Olympic runners ever. He later ranked number one in the world in the mile and 5,000 meters. But he injured himself shortly before the 1972 and 1976 games, preventing his best performance, and he never again competed as an Olympian.

A man of intense self-discipline, Liquori took athletic wins and losses in his stride. His coach at Villanova, the late Jumbo Elliot, was a millionaire business adventurer, Liquori said, who told the runner that running was only a temporary career.

Taking Elliot's advice at face value, Liquori and Jimmy Carnes, a former University of Florida track coach, opened in 1972 the first Athletic Attic store in Gainesville, Florida.

"I saw people jogging, and there was no place to buy good running shoes," Liquori said. He also had observed that people in Europe wore running shoes as casual wear. He predicted that the trend would catch on in the United States.

Today Liquori supervises 142 stores in the United States, New Zealand and Japan, and more than a hundred franchises. Sales total about $40 million, making Athletic Attic the third-largest United States sports shoe chain.

Liquori said, "What we did here is far more difficult than setting a world record."

For the former track star, running bred a need for independence and quick rewards which he found renewed in the excitement of building his chain of stores, a different playing field than track. Liquori said he thinks of himself "as a typical entrepreneur who likes ideas and concepts, and once smooth sailing is achieved, I grow bored."

An individualist like Marty Liquori convinces us of the invincibility of the individual — who, when he discovers the secret of himself, can raise the courage to match the inspiration of Ralph Waldo Emerson, who described the intensified human when he wrote:

I am the owner of the sphere,
Of the seven stars and the solar year,
Of Cæsar's hand and Plato's brain,
Of Lord Christ's heart and
Shakespeare's strain.

If Liquori made the establishment of a chain of successful stores, on top of a starring athletic career, sound easy, it is because knocking down barriers is something he has always liked to do.

"The reason barriers can be made to fall," he said, "is because of plain hard work and dedication to a goal. Find out what you want, go after it, and you'll discover in the process who you are. You may surprise yourself."

Liquori said that he used to tell the story about a lady who went to a concert given by a world-famous violinist. After the concert, she went backstage and said to the artist, "I'd give half my life to be able to play like you did."

The violinist replied, "Madam, I did."

Liquori's point, the point of the story echoed by hundreds of champion athletes and other successful people, is that self-discovery, the child of hard endeavor, opens the way to independence for the individual and an attitude that welcomes change and growth.

Liquori has personified this concept by demonstrating the ability to turn bad news into a new pathway to demonstrate personal excellence. That's what Liquori appears to have done with the discovery a few years ago that he had developed chronic lymphocytic leukemia, which often fails to progress significantly for five or ten years.

The athletic store owner, sports commentator and TV producer learned of the disease after he agreed to become national spokesman for the team-in-training program of the Leukemia Society of America.

The former high school miler, who says he feels no effects from his disease, expects to stay involved in his favorite activities and projects. "More good has come out of this than bad," he observed, proof that challenges in whatever form can provide the keen edge to sharpen the individual's definition of himself.

People like Liquori who are sure of themselves often seem to less certain individuals to be set apart from the crowd. This may be true, but we believe it is because most people lack the analytical tools to describe the big parts that fit together into a whole person. We also believe that the analytical methods explained in this chapter can help you discover the real, total, ultimate you. When you know who you are, you can find the best pathway to your destination. You can say goodbye to oscillation and indecision if they have plagued you in the past.

There can be no overemphasis on the importance of knowing and holding dearly to your personal values. They are the guideposts that line the road of life. Benjamin Franklin, one of America's most distinguished citizens, as a young man wrote a brief description of the thirteen values he prized to guide his life. In his autobiography, Franklin elaborated as to how he periodically reviewed his life to ensure that he was abiding by his self-selected principles. He attributed his great successes to this practice more than any other trait or habit.

Applying Franklin's formula for success, Lyle Nelson here shares a description of the values which guide him. They helped him discover who he was after his awakening at Lake Placid, New York.

Values

1. Character

Integrity is the most important personal characteristic that guides my interactions with others and self. Integrity requires an honest and thorough understanding of myself. Only then can I make commitments that are fair and deliverable to all concerned.

Interactions with others are based on a compassion — a caring — about them. I want to be known for possessing a deep and active compassion for my close friends and an intelligent compassion for humankind.

Decisiveness and enthusiasm are the two traits that will ensure that my talents are put to use.

2. Intellectual Growth

I expose myself to the sources of knowledge that both intrigue me and make me a capable person. I believe that all people are innately geniuses and that it is important to learn hyper-learning skills. By learning in diverse fields, I will develop associative ability to make meaningful discoveries. When I enter the wisdom stage of life, I will be prepared to perpetuate my value to my intimate circle.

3. Personal Health

All my dreams, all my good intentions, all my joy, can be ended if I don't provide them a healthy body to reside in.

I cherish my physical self, not as an object, but as the home of my mental and spiritual energy. What I put into my body, and do to it, is in accordance with this value.

4. Spiritual Growth

I actively explore the purpose of life and seek a deep understanding of what it means to be human — to be alive. I believe that spiritual growth, like physical growth or mental growth, is best achieved by following a plan and committing time and effort to the progress. A sense of spiritual rightness guides every action I take. I don't adjust my spiritual beliefs to fit the situation.

5. Intimacy

I enjoy close, honest and deeply revealing relationships with my blood family and intimate extended family. May I be 100 percent reliable in their times of need. To be a resource to them, I know that I must build my own resources. Across the course of a lifetime, I expect intimacy to be one of my greatest joys and accomplishments.

6. The Environment

To respect the Creator, it is also necessary to respect that which he has created — the environment and the life forms within it. The earth was not made for man to conquer or consume. To the extent possible and practical, I will live in balance with all life and consume with consciousness.

7. Social Contribution

I believe that every person must contribute to making the world a little bit better. My strategy for doing this is to build a healthy self, so that I can build a healthy family, and thereby a better community; and if so chosen, I will carry the message of a healthy world beyond my tight community, but it is community first.

8. Adventure

Although it is beyond my ability to explain to myself, I recognize the great joy derived from mental, spiritual and physical adventures. Whether it's a learned joy or inherited need, periodic adventures which create enthusiasm for life, provide hope, excitement, learning and appreciation for being alive.

9. Financial Growth

I choose to be free of personal financial needs so that my thoughts and actions can turn from survival to flourishing. I know that all the money which I accumulate will ultimately be used to help others and my community.

10. Material Possessions

May I be wise and strong enough to own those things that facilitate my life's purpose. I am comfortable knowing that my home, car, clothes are not extensions or reflections of my true self-worth.

We've constructed a pyramid of personal strengths on the next page. It may be enlightening for you to make your own pyramid and arrange the values listed below in the order of ascending importance to you. Not knowing your values is like standing on slippery ice; everyone can push you around.

My home, possessions
Intimate relationships
Friends and casual relationships

My character
Quest for knowledge and competency
Spiritual growth
Physical health
Need for power and prestige
Contribution to society
Security and finances
Other _____

Highest value

Second-highest values

Third-highest values

Fourth-highest
values

Pyramid of Personal Strength

Envision yourself standing atop this pyramid of personal values. As you grow in wisdom, the hierarchy of your personal values will change.

It is worthwhile for you to study the values listed by Lyle Nelson carefully; then you may wish to make up your own statement of personal values.

The importance of values transmitted from a coach/teacher to students who gain national recognition can

be gauged from the following story of Brad Smith, a basketball coach.

Smith coaches the Oregon City, Oregon, high school
girls' basketball team. It has been rated the best team in
America by *U.S.A. Today* for three consecutive years. In
sixteen years of coaching at the school, leading it to state
championships in 1992 and 1994, Smith has compiled a
winning record of 348 to 66. His philosophy embraces his
fundamental belief that there is a greater scope to life than
the individual can perceive.

"Players," he said, "must realize what their greater
scope in life is, and what they do in athletics must be in
harmony with how they choose to live their lives. If we
don't have high standards to guide us, unconscious disrup-
tion, unconscious friction, are going to sandbag us,
undermine our energy."

Smith observed that if he were to tell a player, "We're
not going to teach values, we're just going to teach basketball," then what he would be saying to that player is, "I
don't care about you. It's okay for you to be just a ship out
there without a rudder, to just float around and whatever
happens, happens.

"Life doesn't work that way. When you choose not to
vote, you are choosing to vote no. I mean, that's how simple
it is. I keep telling the kids that in life you have to take
'stands.' Big or little, it doesn't matter, but at some point
you are going to have to say, 'This is my position'; I won't
budge from it because if I do I will injure my values.

"I think it is impossible to not teach values. Whatever
you do teaches values, either good ones or bad ones."

Smith has little patience for public displays on the
playing fields of nasty tempers, poor self-confidence and
bad manners.

"We are role modeling all the time," he said. "Kids are going to be exactly like we are. If we are in a basketball game and the referee makes a call and I go crazy and scream and yell and do all those crazy things you see on television, how can I not expect my kids to do the same thing when they get a bad call? It's ludicrous of me to expect them to remain calm, possessed of themselves and righteous, with two seconds to go in a game, if I'm ranting and raving about a referee's decision I disagree with."

Smith said that when his team was beaten in a game at Pittsburgh, when his girls went in rated number one and the opposition was rated number two, "The first thing I did when we came into the locker room was to tell the kids, 'They beat us.' The kids knew it. We had a chance to win. They beat us. We didn't lose — they beat us. There's a world of difference. We didn't play poorly, we played good. They played better. Don't give me the fouls, don't give me the hometown, don't give me this or that; they beat us. Next time we beat them. But they beat us this time, and let's deal with it the way it is. Life's like that. Accept defeat, but go up to the bat next time wiser, and more prepared to win."

Bad calls in life should be met with equanimity, Smith believes, referring to a female basketball player who was stricken with a life-threatening disease.

"We had this kid, this six-foot-two-inch sophomore girl, she's a junior this year, potentially an All-American-style kid, who waited for two years as a freshman to play with Tammy Arnold, who is our All-American. When Arnold was suspended last year, the sophomore played three games, averaged eighteen points, fifteen rebounds. I mean this kid is great, going to be a great one. In June of last year she gets multiple sclerosis. Now, that's a bad call. There's nothing she did to deserve that, but she got it. I feel sorry for her; it's a tragedy, but there's nothing that I, her mom and dad, or anyone can do about it.

"Are you going to roll over and feel sorry for yourself and die, or are you going to look and say, 'Hey, I've been dealt a tough blow, but I will deal with it. And I will accept the things that happen, and I will not give in to them.' Whatever happens, happens and you must not give in to feeling sorry for yourself."

We asked Smith the question: "Do you think the spiritual idea, 'I'm very important to God, I'm very important to the universe, I'm a unique individual,' do you think there is a great deal of strength in that?"

Smith replied, "Yes, I think there is a great deal of strength in that if you can convince a kid that she is important, that no matter what else goes wrong around her, she is important, then everything else falls into shape because now she understands. She says to herself, 'I'm important, I have a purpose and if I have a purpose then I must be important.' When she perceives and takes to this idea, then it grows to encompass her place as a unique individual in the universe. Once a person knows this, her future is strong, her self-worth expands, because knowing who you are gives you status and permanence in your own eyes, which reflect God's vision."

Smith observed that his experience with the girls' basketball team has led him to the conclusion that, "The vast majority of us just want to play games; we don't want to do the practice. But the practice is where I get better, and the practice translates into the daily, mundane things that God does to us to make us better people, but we don't want to see those things; we want the big things. You know, we want the great, high experiences. We don't want the low ones. The low experiences are God's way of testing our humility, helping us to forge our character. I see God, and suggest to my kids that God — however they wish to envision Him — is the Master Coach with a great practice plan for each of us. Always there, exactly. He is never going to walk out of practice."

Underestimating Your Qualities

Everyone has some exceptional qualities. We have to understand this and learn to recognize them. We either develop our qualities through our experiences or are born with them. However acquired, we must learn to recognize them because they can carry us to a much higher destiny than we might aspire to otherwise. For example, Lyle Nelson, by not fully realizing his rare physical gifts, settled for just being an Olympic athlete, when perhaps a gold medal was in the cards for him.

There is a touching story that illustrates the idea of not settling for less.

A woman who has died enters heaven and is greeted by St. Peter, who conducts her on a tour. At one place he stops and, above the door, written in gold, is the woman's name.

"This room is mine?" she asks as St. Peter opens the door.

The high angel nods and escorts the woman inside the room, which is filled with marvelous sparkling packages piled high, one on top of the other.

"For me?" the woman asks.

St. Peter nods, but as she rushes forward to claim what is hers, he detains her with the gentle words, "Oh, my dear, these were the unclaimed gifts we had for you on earth."

It should be a littler clearer now that we stunt our growth, we foreshorten what we can be, when we rest from striving, having fulfilled the needs of safety, material possessions, and physical love/sex. And yet, with the accomplishment of these needs, most of us stop, tread water, aimless except for the performance of the minimal work required to stay anchored against the tide.

As we have said, if we truly understand our physiological needs, strengths, limitations, values, attitudes, and aspirations, and how they interact, we can approach the question of: "Who am I?" with greater intelligence.

Here in this chapter, in this book, we have introduced you to men and women who have found themselves and proved by their performances how the heart can soar when it knows its destination. But you won't learn the secret of yourself in a few minutes. It may take years. What we can promise is that if you follow the instructions and exercises in this chapter and the next, you will be on the path to answering "Who am I?"

A word of warning! Once you truly set your feet upon the road to self-illumination, you will never turn away. You may take detours, lag at times, curse the dim light in the darkness that beckons you, but you will be compelled to keep going. The search, once you begin it, is irresistible, and one day, full of yourself and younger than your years, you'll look up, confident of who you are, with stars in your eyes, and believe that the world, and the universe beyond, is no bigger than your soul can be.

5

The Passionate Intuition

There is no greater truth in the world than, "You will become what you think about most." If you are preoccupied with your limitations, these limits will become your ceiling in life. If your thoughts are focused on the physical self, "How do I look? What can I eat? Am I comfortable?" you may experience physical satiation, possibly to the extent that higher-order rewards are excluded.

This chapter develops the theme that champions know they need only one discipline in life, and that is the discipline to control their thoughts, to focus their mental energy on the highest rewards and levels of achievement they wish from life.

To be a champion in life you must see yourself as a fully actualized person. You must focus your thoughts not on what is acceptable; instead, choose the next level higher — the desirable. You will learn in this chapter how to create a workshop in your mind and to project the images that take you to your grandest expectations. You'll learn to reject every thought that will produce a reality less than what you desire. You'll learn that your highest thoughts about yourself are truer than the lowest.

"The meaning of life is ours to create, again and again, for every individual and generation. Only by creating and re-creating the fabric of meaning can we live. We are, of all the species on this planet, the one that lives by the creation of meaning, as bees must manufacture honey or spiders must make the stuff of their webs, spinning vast geometrical landscapes. Thus, there is no single text that can be consulted to find the meaning of life, nor does it exist as a hidden code waiting to be teased out like the sequencing of the human genome. Meaning is what human beings create from what they see and hear and remember, partly private and partly shared within our overlapping lives. Meaning is what we weave with each other and with patterns passed down from the past, selecting, discarding, embroidering, twisting the threads together to draw every man and woman and child into a larger whole."

Mary Catherine Bateson, the American linguist and anthropologist who wrote the words above, captured in lovely prose a definition of the self-actualized person, who was described by Abraham Maslow as the human who has reached the peak of personal expression and excellence. Actually, Bateson makes it clear that truly discovering meaning in life precedes and is a condition of becoming Maslow's self-actualized person.

It was the much-quoted Maslow who defined a hierarchy of human needs as the motivational source for the actions of humans, starting with the most basic physiological demands: food, water and sleep. We progress, he said, upward through safety needs, belonging needs, then esteem needs, and culminate in self-actualization requirements. Self-actualization, Maslow said, is the drawing together of every man, woman and child into a larger whole and is expressed as the highest yearning we humans have for joining our soul with the mystery of the universe.

Maslow outlined a cluster of fourteen characteristics that distinguish self-actualized individuals. In summary, these characteristics, or values, define individuals who are accepting of themselves and others, are relatively independent of the culture or society in which they live, and are somewhat detached, but have very close personal ties to a few other people, and they are deeply committed to solving problems which they deem to be important. Also, self-actualized individuals appreciate intensely simple or natural events such as a lovely starry night. Maslow described such an evening as a "peak experience." This and other peak experiences to which he referred often involved the momentary loss of self feelings, replaced with transcendence. Athletes have described these feelings as being "in the zone."

Reports of peak experiences also include the feeling of limitless horizons opening up and of being simultaneously very powerful, yet weak. Peak experiences are extremely positive in nature and often cause an individual to change the direction of his or her future behavior, Maslow believed. He also believed that everyone is capable of having peak experiences, but he thought that self-actualized persons have such experiences more frequently.

Part of the process of self-actualization comes from identifying your personal strengths. Once you do so, you can begin to build them into assets which will enrich your life more than you know. The following exercises have been designed to help you discover your personal strengths. As you learn your personal strengths and build on them, the courage to investigate new dimensions of yourself is developed. Courage comes from learning and putting your strengths to work.

In the previous chapter we discussed briefly that most people underestimate their qualities and, as a result, settle for less than they are capable of achieving. Qualities and personal strengths may be said to be synonymous, but, in any case, each individual who desires to make the most of himself needs to examine his personal assets and his weaknesses to improve his effectiveness as a human being. Inevitably, such self-examination brings about the revelation that takes the individual a step higher in his evolution toward personal excellence.

Identification of Personal Strengths

On the next few pages you will discover some exercises that are interesting to do. Find a pad of paper, copy the exercises, and fill in the answers.

Select three different successes of which you are particularly proud and three activities you enjoy. Then fill in the strengths that are relevant to each. The strengths/skills listed most frequently are those waiting to be developed.

1.   One of my greatest successes was _____.
      The skills making this success possible were:
      1.
      2.
      3.

2. One of my greatest successes was _____.
    The skills making this success possible were:
    1.
    2.
    3.

3. One of my greatest successes was _____.
    The skills making this success possible were:
    1.
    2.
    3.

Favorite Activities

1. One of the activities I enjoy most in life is:
    _____. The skills inherent in this activity are:
    1.
    2.
    3.

2. One of the activities I enjoy most in life is:
    _____. The skills inherent in this activity are:
    1.
    2.
    3.

3. One of the activities I enjoy most in life is:
    _____. The skills inherent in this activity are:
    1.
    2.
    3.

4.   Based on the successes I've identified at this
      time in my life, my top five strengths appear to
      be:
      1.
      2.
      3.
      4.
      5.

(You should be able to identify at least twelve
different strengths. Strengths could include those listed
below. Choose the ones that fit you and make a check
mark.)

Attention to detail.
Good planner.
Know myself well.
Good listener.
A knack for discovering creative solutions.
Physical energy.
Have a way with written words.
Effective verbal communicator.
I make other people feel valuable.
Expansive knowledge base in my field.
Great cook/entertainer.
Good family manager.
Others you can think of:

_____

_____

_____

_____

_____

Just as it is important for you to identify your personal strengths, so is it important to pinpoint your weaknesses.

Identification of Personal Weaknesses

Everybody has weaknesses. There is nothing surprising about that, but you can contribute to them by not recognizing them. Having recognized them — specifically those which impede you from reaching your destiny — then doing nothing to improve them is laziness.

So often our weaknesses are products of our self-talk. "I can't write," or "I hate to write," and they remain weaknesses or dislikes until we change our self-talk. While individual strengths take on a great variety of talents, it's interesting that the weaknesses that block most people from reaching their potential are quite universal. They are:

1. Inability to hold focus/vision.
   a) Giving in to the more immediate reward.
   b) Becoming overextended by minutiae, majoring in minors.
2. Failure to plan: "No one plans to fail; they fail to plan."
3. Talking themselves out of the greatness within.
4. Lack of communication skills to convey their wants and persuade others to assist them.
5. Unwillingness to ask for help — advice, coaching, physical assistance — when it is needed.

Recognizing Detrimental Patterns

Weaknesses often take the form of patterns of behavior, which, if recognized, can be changed for more positive actions.

Here are examples of patterns (habits) that do not serve the purpose of the individual:

"I get upset when someone in front of me drives slowly."

"I get defensive when I am criticized or offered advice."

"Every morning I wake up worried about my responsibilities."

"I accept the way things are, and do not look for solutions."

"I let interruptions distract me, and do not finish my work."

List three detrimental patterns which you would like to change.

1. _____

2. _____

3. _____

Circle Your Willingness to Change

```
|_____|_____
 -5   -4   -3   -2   -1   0   +1   +2   +3   +4   +5
```

How to Change Detrimental Patterns

There are three major strategies for changing detrimental patterns. They are:

1. Change the environment which induces the detrimental pattern.
2. Associate with people who have positive patterns.
3. Create favorable experiences using new, positive patterns.

If you review your strengths, you will notice that many of them reflect positive attitudes and habits you possess. Much of our behavior is accomplished on autopilot. For example, we don't need to think when someone compliments us. Out of habit we say, "Thanks," or deny the compliment with, "Aw, shucks, anybody could have done it better."

Such answers are habits of which we may not even be aware. It is this lack of awareness, this lack of seeing ourselves as who we have become, that can create problems as we design a life that is best for us.

It is not productive to dwell on our shortcomings, and certainly they need not define the future for us. But certainly, if we do not try to improve our deficiencies, then our present shortcomings will in fact define our future.

Habits are the repetition of behavior that once served us well — we got the results we wanted — but now they may be no longer effective. For example, it is healthy for babies to get cranky when hungry. But as adults, we don't need to become cranky, and crankiness does not put food on the table anymore.

We have listed several prevalent attitudes and habits (our automatic behavior patterns) which hinder most of us from reaching our destiny. It will be valuable for you to recognize similar shortcomings you might have.

Recognizing Your Attitudes and Habits

The quality of our lives is determined more by the decisions we make — or fail to make — than by any other factors. More influential than the wealth we were born into, our color of skin, innate intelligence, physical size, gender (or whatever else you may choose to pinpoint as a determinant of your life) are the decisions we make concerning what we're going to do with what we've got. Thousands of people have started with far less than we have and achieved feats that still echo in history. Of course, we know the stories of the historically famous like Abraham Lincoln and George Washington, but what about those more common persons whose stubbornness wins a prize or goal for them because they understand what Willa Cather meant when she wrote about artistic growth, meaning the growth of honesty and the soul: "Artistic growth is common more than it is anything else, a refining of the sense of truthfulness. The stupid believe that to be truthful is easy; only the artist, the great artist, knows how difficult it is."

Stephen Charles Fonyo, a one-legged man, was like an artist who created a triumph of himself. He is an example of a person emerging from a childhood of pain, ridicule and scorn from his schoolmates in Vernon, British Columbia, because he had only one leg. Yet his handicap did not stop him from completing a torturous 8,000-kilometer cross-country Canadian marathon against cancer.

An article in Canada's *MacLean's Magazine* described Fonyo:

"Looking tanned and self-confident, the 19-year-old one-legged runner completed his 8,000-kilometer journey for lives in a driving rainstorm in Victoria. After hobbling onto a rocky cliffside overlooking his final destination, Fonyo strode down a paved pathway to a red-carpeted ramp that jutted into the water. Accompanied by his parents, Stephen Sr. and Anna, and his sister Suzanne, Fonyo dipped his artificial left leg into the icy waters of the Pacific Ocean."

"With that, the applause and cheers from a crowd of 6,000 crested over the young man who determinedly jogged out of obscurity to become a hero. Exalted a beaming Fonyo as he turned to hug his family: 'Yahoo! It's finally over.' Fonyo's lonely run began fourteen months ago in St. Johns, spanned ten provinces, and, by the time it was over, had raised over nine million dollars for the Canadian Cancer Society. On the road, Fonyo used up six artificial legs and suffered blisters on his right foot and painful shinsplints in his right leg. As he headed toward mile zero on the Trans-Canadian Highway in Victoria last week, Fonyo was visibly in pain. He had been prescribed painkillers, he explained, but 'I forgot to take them today.'

"In the course of his 425-day journey Fonyo ran through sub-zero weather during the prairie winter and humid heat as he entered the British Columbia interior. At the start of his run Fonyo regularly covered thirty-two kilometers a day with only a howling wind and a few cars for companionship. Then, as he headed for the finish line last week, there were cheering fans and public idol worship to help him on his way."

Another Canadian, Kate Pace, convinced herself while preparing for the World Alpine Ski Championships in 1993 that she could beat her opponents with one hand behind her back. That brash conviction was born of necessity: Her broken left wrist, the result of a crash during a race just three weeks previously, was in a cast that prevented her from using both poles to push out of the gate atop Mount Kotakakura in Morioka, Japan.

But twenty-four-year-old Pace said she had decided that, despite her injury, the World Championship was her race, her course and her gold medal. Starting seventeenth, Pace one-armed her way out of the gate and used her exceptional gliding technique to build a lead on the flatter portions of the course.

She crossed the finish line fractions of a second ahead of Anja Haas of Austria, her then-nearest competitor.

"No one can touch me now," she said, and in a glorious week for Canada's Woman Skiers, no one did.

As both of these determined young people demonstrated, the art of living is to make good decisions so that the journey of life is both enjoyable and fruitful. This thought was captured by the famous Japanese scholar and translator of Zen Buddhist texts, D.T. Suzuki, who said, "I am an artist at work — my work of art is my life."

To excel at this art — to turn your life's journey into a masterpiece — you need to know the two pieces of information anyone planning a journey must have: One, what's the starting point? and two, where am I going? The starting point in planning your life is to answer the question, "Who am I right now?" The destination is who you wish to be at the other end of the journey. Every step you take in the process, the steps that transform you from who you are to who you will ultimately become, requires a decision — a choice. It is the accumulation of choices, good or bad, that makes your life the success you wish and are capable of producing, or a failure in your own mind.

The Workshop of the Mind

One excellent method to help you transform yourself from who you are to who you can become is known as the Workshop of the Mind. This is a special place you create in your mind from which we will show you how to originate, organize and direct marvelous powers of concentration. You will be able to project your thoughts from dream wishes into reality. Before we describe the Workshop of the Mind, it is important for us to acknowledge Alexander Everett, the spiritual leader and thinker who originated the Workshop of the Mind as part of his spiritual growth program, Inward Bound. You will meet Alexander Everett in a later chapter, and you'll find the way he thinks fascinating and inspirational.

Alexander originated the Workshop of the Mind as a remarkable method by which people can build a sort of "mental forge" with which to shape thoughts into powerful projectiles that can accomplish specific objectives.

Actually, as an idea, the Workshop of the Mind is similar to the workplaces most of us use in our daily activities. A physician has an office with medical equipment; a mechanic uses a garage equipped with his various automotive tools; an architect furnishes his office with a drafting board and the instruments to measure elevations, angles and distances. The point is, as in the case of your workday office, you need to furnish your Workshop of the Mind with the tools and resources you will need to create images of your future; and when you outfit the Workshop of the Mind to create these images, you can bring much leeway and imagination to bear.

Also, as you will see in the following explanation, the location of your Workshop of the Mind is important.

Following is the way for you to build your own Workshop of the Mind:

First, visualize a peaceful outdoor scene, perhaps one you have visited many times. When you come into this scene, it's always peaceful and you experience tranquility. All of the concerns of the everyday world drop away when you enter your special place in nature. For one of the authors, Thorn Bacon, his special place, one that lives in his memory, is a small hollow, surrounded by grasses and trees, where shadows play upon the surface of a small, deep pond where fishes glide. A gnarled cypress bends over the slow-running water and is the home of two lazy bronze copper-heads who drape themselves sinuously along the trunk of the tree and sleep through the drowsy Texas afternoons.

Whenever Bacon felt the world was too much, he would slip away with a fishing pole, ostensibly to cast for the catfish and bass that lurked in the pond on Cibolo Creek. Actually, Bacon spent his fishing time daydreaming and was surprised when the cork bobber on his line tipped the end of his rod, indicating interest below in the worm squirming on his hook.

The Yellow Door

Long after Bacon left Texas and Cibolo Creek behind, visions of the pond in summer, fall and winter came back to him — always as restorative memories: leaves turning crisp in autumn, a sharp clarity in the air from the wind washing the trees with sprinkles of hard, cold rain; clever, cautious pheasants with their crackling calls stalking in the tall grasses, and the hawks ascending higher on the blue, swollen air to search sharp-eyed for squirrels hurrying with their winter nesting chores.

When Bacon learned about the Workshop of the Mind from Alexander Everett, he reconstructed the pond at Cibolo Creek as his scene from nature. Then, according to Alexander's instructions, in his mind he built a secret house on a hill overlooking the pond. It was a cottage hidden in a copse of trees with a clear view of the pond. A yellow door opened into the house.

Yellow, Alexander explained, is the color of the mind. Thus, the yellow door signified the entrance to a place of mental activity. In Alexander's program, where Bacon first learned about the Workshop of the Mind, the spiritual teacher emphasized that the appearance and construction of the secret house varies from person to person.

Furnishing the house is a matter of personal taste, just so long as several objects are present. They are:

1. A table on which there is a telephone, a computer or a fax … some type of instrument from which the individual can communicate his thoughts.

2. Books or audio or video tapes containing all the knowledge in the universe are to be found in the house.

3. On one wall hangs a picture of the owner of the house. A bright light shines on the picture, which displays the individual at his best.

4.   At the other end of the room there is a movie
        screen with a bright light shining on it. A clock
        rests on a table and a calendar hangs from one
        wall.

The Workshop of the Mind, Alexander explained,
takes place in the secret house which, as we've said, each
person designs to his own taste and comfort. For example,
one person the authors encountered furnished his workshop
with rich and expensive rugs, wall hangings, and objets
d'art. Exotic Eastern perfumes of sandalwood and rose
petals made a heady fragrance in the room.

Bacon's own workshop resembles a comfortable
English library with leatherbound books overflowing from
tall shelves that adorn the high walls of the room. There is
the congenial clutter on tables, desks and reading stands
typical of the absentminded writer. It is a cheerful, meditative room, and the compatible visitor could easily become
lost in the friendly ambience of trustworthy literature whose
niches in the writings of the world are announced by the
sturdy titles beaming from the spines of the treasured
volumes standing at attention row after row.

The great value of the Workshop of the Mind is that it
quickly becomes the designated place where you go to
express the best of yourself and to concentrate on the
personal dreams you want to become reality by picturing
them in accomplished form on the movie screen you have
installed in your Workshop of the Mind. From the
workshop, the individual can communicate with the whole
of the universe. There are no limitations.

The screen at one end of the room is used by the
workshop's occupant to display his dreams, wishes or
projects. As the individual projects his thoughts on the

screen, they take form just like scenes which appear sequentially in the mind in a sleep-dream. The difference is that the person is projecting wishes for the fulfillment of a project dear to him.

Let us suppose that your dream is to be the head of a mechanical engineering firm which has earned a formidable reputation for building difficult bridges in Third World countries. But you are young, inexperienced, with an engineering diploma and no accomplishments in bridge design to recommend you for employment.

How would you picture yourself on your movie screen? In other words, what dominant image representing your wish would you first create and transfer to the screen? Would it be one in which you are portrayed in a bush jacket and helmet, with blueprints tucked under your arm, giving instructions to a native strawboss as to where workers must start digging to create the foundation for pilings that will support the bridge structure when it is erected?

Dreams you project onto your movie screen must be accurate if they are to come true, and they can be in stages. For example, in the image described above details are important. How old have you made yourself? Your age in your dream image is important because it indicates when in your life you may expect the image to become reality. In what country is the bridge-building located? What language is spoken?

Why are such details important? Because the energy of the universe, always available to help us achieve the passion that is dear to us, requires us to define it with exactitude.

Lyle Nelson, the four-time Olympian co-author of this book, learned the truth about exactness in wishes when his own dream of achieving status as an Olympic athlete did not characterize him as an Olympic medal winner. As a youth, he dreamed of joining the worldwide fraternity of Olympians — which came true — but he never furnished his dream with a picture of himself as a biathlon champion standing on the winner's podium with a gold, silver or bronze medal suspended by a ribbon from his neck.

The Workshop of the Mind can help you visualize the accomplishment of your passion. And as you construct pictures of yourself on your movie screen, doing things that excite and fulfill you, it is easy to add details until you feel satisfied that the image you have projected is complete.

By revisiting the Workshop of the Mind on a regular basis, the dream you want to accomplish grows more real, authentic and stronger, until finally you can turn it into reality. Remember, your unconscious mind does not know the difference between a visualization that is vividly enacted and reality. If it continues to get the same image-message, it will act to help to make that dream come true.

A final word about the Workshop of the Mind: it is remarkably versatile. The dream wishes you hope to convert into reality do not have to be "big" in scope for them to happen. But the mind is so powerful — because it draws upon the unlimited reservoir of power in the energy of the universe — that it may accomplish what seem to be miracles. This was the case as reported by renowned cancer specialist Dr. Carl Simonton, who wrote about patients in his treatment program in his book, *Getting Well Again.*

One of Simonton's patients was a sixty-one-year-old man with extensive throat cancer. Through his use of mental imagery and radiation therapy, he was healed after eighteen months. In the course of his remission, he drew pictures to represent the dwindling of his disease. Dr. Simonton was amazed to observe how accurately the man described his cancer's size and shape. The man seemed to see internally what Dr. Simonton could only observe with an instrument. After his cancer was gone, the man used the mental techniques he had learned to eliminate arthritis and sexual impotence.

There are thousands of men and women who have effectively used some form of the Workshop of the Mind to transform themselves. If such transformative power, which has been expressed in many beneficial ways, can be guided by ordinary individuals, then the range of our capabilities seems to be extraordinary. But the secret now, as it has always been, is to believe, without doubt or insincere conviction, that we as individuals may, at will, tap into the vast reservoir of power that lights the moon, ignites the sun, and moves the stars. It provides us with the imagination to surpass our own small needs, to see beyond them, to behold our brightness as a direct reflection of that mysterious power.

The self-clarifying exercises in this chapter and the Workshop of the Mind are intended to provide you with the information you need to make good decisions for yourself. Frequently, a shortage of courage, rather than information, cuts off the pathway to an advancing life. That's okay to admit; courage doesn't come by prescription. It comes — as we pointed out earlier — from learning your strengths and weaknesses. And creating courageous decisions for the future of your life cannot be made, we believe, with great sensitivity and intelligence, if you don't believe in the divine wisdom of the universe.

If you believe the universe was created with a plan, that it has intelligence that perpetuates its existence, then you can also understand that we, as living entities, are somehow a part of that plan. This idea is undeniable, and for proof of it we merely have to look at any life form in nature to discover that if it lacks a plan or reason to continue, ultimately it will decay, lose its energy, and come to rest. That is the law of entropy — all systems without an outside influx of energy tend toward disorder and inertness.

To ensure our survival, each of us must have a reason to exist — not necessarily an external reason — but an internal one that gives us the incentive to continue. That incentive is joy. It is the built-in sensation that propels us forward as individuals and as a species. We all desire a life that brings deep joy, and the greatest joy is that which simultaneously soothes the body, mind and soul. Such a life is obtainable, and occasionally we get a glimpse of it in peak experiences such as we have described in these pages. Such deep, brief experiences bring about the feeling the great poet Wordsworth described when he wrote: "One in whom persuasion and belief has ripened into faith, and faith become a passionate intuition."

Although we know this joy is there for us — the passionate intuition — and we know we possess the courage and commitment to make decisions, we still may not see the pathway to our enlightened life. This is perhaps the purest use of the word enlightenment. "Enlightenment" means to be shown the way to pure joy.

Enlightenment is not a term restricted to those who have found the religiously correct way; it best describes a person who can see his personal pathway to pure joy. This pathway penetrates the forest of "Who am I?" and deposits you eventually at the destination of enlightenment. But many of us are impatient for enlightenment; we struggle to force an answer to the quintessential questions "Who am I?" "Where am I headed?" How can we make good decisions for ourselves, we ask, decisions that bring us joy, if the answers evade us? The solution is not simple, but if you really dare to open yourself to who you are, if you stop resisting the "passionate intuition" which is waiting inside you for your full acknowledgment, the information you seek will come to you like the opening of a tulip. It's that simple. Certainly, awareness does not always come in a flash of light, but it can be achieved if you prepare yourself — like a garden waiting to bloom — with the tools of self-discovery we have provided in this and the previous chapter.

In every way, you are the artist who creates himself — "A work of art in progress," and your decision of who you can be can be bolstered and steadied if you take to heart the progress others have made to define and refine themselves. The "Characteristics of Champions" found at the end of this chapter are achievable ideals against which to measure your progress.

A final word: There is an inevitable logic about accepting the belief that you have a destiny beyond your body. All the signs of nature in the universe that surround us tells us this is so. It is a practical reality. You can influence your destiny, but that does not alter the fact that you have a destiny. To be without one is not to exist. Bernie Siegal, surgeon and popular author of *Love, Medicine and Miracles,* insists that each of us is a torchbearer responsible for burning as bright as we can, and handing our flame on:

"As the poet said: Life is no brief candle, but a torch to be held high before passing it along to future generations. I believe we are all here to be bright torches that light one another's way. We are here to use our lives and burn up — not burn out. We must find our own particular way of loving the world and put our energy into it. Decide your way of loving and you will be rewarded."

Joe Vigil, the world's foremost running coach, who trains athletes in Alamosa, Colorado's high, thin air, was adamant about the idea of a person knowing himself as an absolute forerunner to success in the competitive fast-moving world of today.

"You know," Vigil said, "I think the standards of the world today are so high that there are certain things you are going to have to do to meet and exceed them. Number one, I believe, people, athletes or not, are going to have to learn to focus more than they've ever had to focus in their life, and at a higher level than Americans are used to. Number two — they are going to have to develop new environments to learn and train in because the ones we have now are not supportive. Also, I think we're going to have to get in touch with ourselves more, call it the spiritual if you wish, but I call it mental energy, and we have to learn how to tap into that energy whether it's spiritual or otherwise. So those three things are of key importance: focus, environment and mental energy. Then and only then will we be able to compete and perform at a higher level to meet the standards of the world beyond us, beyond American waters."

We asked Joe Vigil what he does to help an athlete who comes to him without a philosophy of life.

He said, "Yes, I have a philosophy, and I present it to them. We go over it together, and I discover that most of the people who come to us often have never had an opportunity to delve into life because they're constantly bombarded by superficial things. By things that are external to their goals. You know, everything is measured today in terms of materialism: Nice-looking cars, nice-looking girls, nice-looking sports jackets. Everything is objective, but often those who come here don't have the power of abstraction, the ability to discern real value, because they've never been taught. Our educational system does not provide for it. I'm sure there are exceptions and there are some good teachers out there.

"There is tremendous creativity that goes untapped because we don't give ourselves a chance to get in tune with ourselves. I tell the kids that they have to be by themselves for at least an hour a day to figure out what they really want out of life and what they want out of their sport and how they want to use their God-given skills to achieve what they're thinking about. And we talk about higher power and I believe they can tap into this power because the aura of electricity is around each and every one of us, and it's there to be utilized. You see it in competition when a person is really in tune with himself."

Norm Bellingham, Olympic gold medalist kayaker, Harvard graduate, former employee of the United States Olympic Committee for research on principles of excellence as they pertain to sports, told us how he found himself during his own pursuit of excellence and how he emerged from a gold-medal performance with an understanding of how the spirit of performance can transcend the idea of winning and lift the participants to an inspiring unity of spirit.

"The 1984 Olympics was a disappointing experience for me, but the international competition in Europe that season exposed me to the level of excellence that the East Germans and Russians had achieved, and it awoke in me a desire to reach their level and extend the sport to levels yet unknown. Another year of training in Lake Placid, New York, left me still pretty frustrated and actually sick with Epstein-Barr Virus. Finally, I couldn't put off any longer what I had come to realize when I was at the 1984 Olympics: To become the best — no, even more important than that — to develop a sport in a new dimension of excellence, I would have to do a mentorship with the best in my sport."

Bellingham said he thought the best training methods in kayaking were being used by New Zealanders, so he called Ian Ferguson who had won three gold medals, and asked permission to train with him and his partner, Paul McDonald, the winner of two gold medals.

"I'm not sure why he said yes," Bellingham observed. "Paul McDonald picked me up at the airport and they put me up at Ian's house, gave me a boat and loaned me a bike until I could find a flat to stay in. They really helped me out a great deal. Their support was unsolicited, and I was certainly warmly received. They took me under their wings and, well, they mentored me. They saw the relationship as mutually beneficial. The fact that I had begun to improve so much and kept up with them in training was the proof they needed that their unorthodox approach to kayak training was a good system. I actually beat them on occasion, and I think they actually took enjoyment in my progress."

"What impressed me was how they went after each session with such incredible intensity and passion. Yes, that's the word, passion. For anyone who didn't have the same internal drive, their methods were too demanding."

Bellingham said that the New Zealand environment, the closeness, the exertion, the spirit of friendly competition, produced a feeling that was almost an "out-of-body" experience which forced the development in him of stronger character.

"It was almost as if I could view myself from an out-of-body position. I could actually begin to see who I was more clearly than ever before, and sometimes that was good and sometimes it wasn't so good, but I knew I could work and what was happening to me was in the form of a trans-formation."

Bellingham said he was amazed that his body, actually the whole human organism with which he worked, was coming close to achieving the state of excellence he had only dreamed about.

"I grew up thinking," he said, "that the real jocks were Olympic gods, like Ian Ferguson, and that the light around them glowed. It was easy to be humble; everyone around me in New Zealand already had a gold medal. But I started seeing myself in a different way. I was making the boat move fast. The plan of taking my sport to a higher level of action was actually happening."

Bellingham's return to the United States was greeted, the athlete said, with resentment from the United States team, "who seemed to be chaffed that I had chosen to train without them, or maybe I was just an outsider when I arrived. As it turned out, I had to beat Greg Barton, then America's best kayaker in the 500 meters, to win a spot on the World Championship Team. No one from the United States was in support of me, and I could hear the whole dock of officials on the United States team yelling, 'Go Greg.' Fortunately, the New Zealanders were training in Lake Placid, and they had heard about my plight. In a race I had with him, Greg got a better start than I did, but I passed him 100 meters into the race, and with 400 meters to go I felt like I was going to stomp him. I have to admit I was more upset with the officials who seemed to be on his side than I was with him. I was almost beating him out of anger. Then I began to hear: 'Go Norm, go Norm.' There, on the dock, along the course, were the four Kiwi guys yelling at the top of their lungs for me."

Bellingham said that he and Greg Barton patched up their differences and were teammates in the 1,000 meters double contest during the 1988 Olympics.

"During the Olympics, our chief competition was the East Germans and the New Zealanders — the latter, the very people I had idolized when I started this sport. And throughout the race it was the New Zealanders and us — Greg and me — who vied for the gold. They got off to a faster start. I could see them in front of us, but we were able to pass them the last 100 meters or so."

Bellingham said he remembered feeling very guilty on the awards stand with he and Barton standing above the New Zealanders. Then Ian Ferguson's wife came up to Bellingham as soon as she and the others were able to break through the crowd after the medal ceremony. Tears were streaming down her face, and Norman said he thought, "Oh, God, she was expecting her husband Ian to win, even though he had actually won a gold medal the day before in the doubles. But I thought, here she's going to tell me congratulations and I'm going to see that she's absolutely miserable. But she came up and gave me the biggest hug and told me she screamed for me the whole last 250 meters."

"Can you imagine that? Our boats were side by side, her husband's and mine, and Ian's wife was cheering me, because in a roundabout way, I was one of them. Ian and the others understood her enthusiasm, and we were all pretty much in tears as she congratulated me. There are some people you are united with, and when they win, you win."

Bellingham's discovery that day was a depth of feeling that gave him an insight into himself, into who he was, which was very much like Wordsworth's "passionate intuition."

Characteristics of Champions

From our discussions with so many champions in the preparation of this book, we thought distilling those traits universal (or nearly so) to all the champions would be extremely valuable and interesting. The list is certainly worth adopting for every person who seeks self-discovery and strives to develop personal excellence.

Champions:

- create an environment that supports winning.
- step outside the system periodically to get a fresh look to be sure the system is the best possible for producing the desired outcome.
- believe that effort outperforms natural talent.
- surround themselves with positive forces and seek to associate with the best.
- give away energy and love because it comes back multiplied (this quality is not universal to all our champs).
- have an inspiring dream.
- expect to win, and then discover how.
- take one manageable step at a time.
- see excellence as an ongoing process, measured periodically by a test event, to ensure that the process is working.
- don't let "unfair treatment" deter them.
- are outrageously themselves.
- don't waste mental energy building defense mechanisms and excuses.
- understand the essential element of each task.
- discover where their passion lies and then follow that path.
- have learned a way to clear their mind.
- see the bigger picture.
- all have a sense of urgency (value of time) — do it now.
- are good losers but don't like to lose.

- all use affirmations.
- give a part of the victory to those who help them achieve it. They show gratitude.

Connecting Daily Deeds with Eternal Purpose

Thomas Morris, the philosopher who teaches the meaning of life at the University of Notre Dame, has given a definition of purpose that illuminates the "passionate intuition" of Wordsworth with clarity and a sense of the ultimate destination:

"We are here to attempt to give more to this life than we take from it, a task that, if undertaken properly, is impossible. The more we give, the more we get. But that's the point.

"We are here to discover, develop and cultivate, in loving stewardship of our world, our neighbors and ourselves. Each of us is intended to grow and flourish within the power of our talents on every dimension of worldly existence: the Intellectual, the Aesthetic and the Moral — the great I AM — in such a way as to find our place in the overarching realm of the Spiritual, the ultimate context of it all.

"There is more to life than meets the eye. Much is required. But more is offered. We are participants in a grand enterprise, not called upon to consume with endless desire, but rather to care and create in such a way as to free the spirit of this vast creation to love and glorify its creator forever.

"Why? Because it's good. And that's good enough for me."

6

Passion is the Fuel of High Achievement

In many subliminal ways we have heard the message, "Now, dear, don't set your expectations too high; you will be disappointed when you don't get what you want." Inherent in this message is the advice to "hold back a bit; don't commit wholeheartedly" as a means of protecting yourself. What is it we restrain when we hold back? It is our passion we restrain. Too many of us have been taught to suppress our natural passion. No greater loss is there than to lose our passion for daily life.

In this chapter you will see the results that champions produce when they allow their passion to be the fuel for their motivation. Passion isn't an emotion gone out of control; it is the fierce desire that directs our energy to uncommon achievements. As such, passion, taken to its heights, is like a holy fire that consumes and releases the exalted spirit in the flame of high endeavor.

Writing centuries ago that, "passion is a sort of fever in the mind," William Penn could not have found a person who more perfectly modeled his description of the burning force that motivates human accomplishment than Marilyn King.

She is the remarkable two-time Olympic pentathlete, the first woman to hold the job of track and field coach at the University of California at Berkeley, whose performance at the 1980 Olympic trials has never been fully appreciated. Passion is the only word to describe how Marilyn King, with a seriously injured back that prevented her from doing any physical training whatsoever (she could not even sit up straight), so intensely concentrated her "fever of the mind" that she won second place in the Olympic trials for the pentathlon.

King's story started in 1979, when she decided to prepare herself for the 1980 Olympic trials by emulating the training model gold medalist Bruce Jenner established for himself to win the pentathlon at the 1976 Olympics. Actually, King's interest in track and field dates back to her sophomore days in high school at Staten Island, New York. When she became Eastern States pentathlon champion, one of three girls who competed for the title, she got hooked and, "never looked back." Eventually, she was chosen to represent the East at a national championship competition in California. From the participants, the United States Olympic Committee chose several girls to admit to the Olympic training camp. Smarting because she was not picked when she knew she was the better athlete, and proved it by outperforming one of the girls who had been selected, Marilyn flew home with the hard-core knowledge that someday she would compete in the Olympics.

King's conviction was so solid, so absolute, that she was unable to find a place in her mind for any conflicting doubt. Before California, she had not thought of herself as a top contender in track and field events. Now, she knew she had the "right stuff." Also, she had discovered the principle of winning, which she would teach to other athletes and corporate executives twenty years later.

"By daring to imagine something that seemed outrageous of accomplishment — winning a place on the Olympic team — my mind created images of me being chosen. Since your mind can't handle two conflicting images at the same time, like winning and losing, I resolved to concentrate on the positive one, the one that pictured me as a victorious Olympian," King said.

She was not to understand how powerful this strategy would become in her life until much later when — incapacitated with an injured spine — she was to apply it in an amazing imagery process that was to turn a vision of athletic success into a physical performance which actually matched the anticipated accomplishments she imagined.

True to her self-prediction, King participated in the pentathlete events at the 1972 Olympics in Munich, and again four years later in Montreal.

While King made her dream of being an Olympic competitor come true, she, like Lyle Nelson and many others, thrilled to have achieved the high status, did not win a medal in 1972 or 1976. The reason, she said, was that, "Instead of visualizing myself as the winner of the pentathlon, my mental image was of me walking into the Olympic stadium as a proud contender. All I had to do to get a rush was to bring up my dream and I'd get excited. I saw myself decked out in Olympic colors, walking with other Olympic athletes.

"I did not," she said, "ever project my imagination beyond being an Olympic participant. I never once pictured myself winning. Never once did I image the gun going off in the 100-meter hurdles and me crossing the finish line ahead of the pack."

It wasn't until later, King explained, that she understood, "You get exactly what you envision, not what you intend. To win," she said, "you must match your intention with your vision. That's what I did during the Olympic trials in 1980. I came in second."

It was in 1980, the year that would mark the third time King would compete in the Olympic trials, that her automobile was struck from behind by a truck. An ordinary person injured as badly as she was — a damaged disk in her spine — might have given up the dream of winning the Olympic trials. Not King! Despite a band of pain that ran from the back of her head down to her heels from the bulging disk in her spine, she decided to train for her trials in an unorthodox fashion. Since she could not turn her body over, sit up, stand, or put any weight-bearing pressure on her spine, and she certainly couldn't sprint and do the vigorous physical training necessary to put her in top condition for the trials, King decided to train in her mind. She would prop herself up in a chair in front of her television and watch videotapes of top Olympic pentathlon winners. Far beyond merely observing these athletes in action, King made it her goal to memorize the outstanding assets each superior performer displayed on the screen. Not only did she commit to memory the winning configuration of each athlete, but superimposed the exact pattern and sequence of movements — run, jump, hurdle, shot put — of the performing athlete on her own image of herself replacing him or her in action. She emulated in her imagination each winning performance, imprinting on her mind and muscles a faultless replication of the athlete's virtuosity on the playing field. By the time King's back had healed — still tender but the pain largely gone — King had spent more than 500 hours studying the images of champion athletes in action on video format. She rejected some champions as role models because she detected in their performances flaws she did not want to absorb into her own winning technique.

When she was able to walk, she went to the track where she would actually perform; and there, with a friend who set up the events she would have to perform in her trials, she spent hours projecting mental visions of herself running, jumping, or throwing the shot put. While many athletes plan championship assaults on a sport, King's dedication to imaging her performance was a masterpiece of patience and scrupulous detail. By the time her June 1980 Olympic trials arrived, she had competed — in her mind — on the track and field at least a thousand times.

We asked King if she thought her intense visualization and mental rehearsals actually caused a thought-inspired physical adaptation of her muscles? In other words, did her muscles adjust, grow, physiologically change, as a result of the power of suggestion from her mind?

King answered: "I don't know if my muscles grew, if they were tempered and formed by my mental power to perform as if they'd been trained in the field. I do know that if you take someone who has a leg injury and you have him or her do an exercise with the good leg, and then you have him envision the same exercise on the injured leg, we know that under these circumstances there are neurological firings in the muscles. Whether muscles are being built in this process, I don't know. What I am clear about in my own case is that neurological firings were present in my muscles as I concentrated for hundreds of hours, envisioning the events I would compete in. I wound up competing in the Olympic trials of 1980, never having trained physically, never having come out of the starting block, never having gone over the high jump bar, never having worked on my steps in the long jump, and we're talking about some highly technical events. It's one thing to be in the high jump and to be able to jump high, but you have to get yourself directly over the bar, not one inch in or one inch out, and that takes a lot of training. Physical training. And I wasn't able to do that physical training, yet I placed second at the Olympic trials." King's achievement seems to indicate strongly that the passion to win — the "fever in the mind" — coupled with powerful, repetitive mental imagery, can produce astonishing physical performances without practice.

Arnold Schwarzenegger, one of the great body builders of the 1970s, was once described as planning the kind of physique he wanted to achieve, then sculpting his body to match his artistic mental conceptions. First he imagined what he wanted to achieve, then he focused on that image during his workouts. The whole process was begun and maintained by the image of his inner eye.

There is no question, and there is growing evidence to support the idea, that the mind can affect the body in dramatic ways.

King said her performance on the two days of her Olympic trials was the same sort of experience that happens when an aroused mother picks up an automobile by its bumper to rescue her daughter from the vehicle's wheels. King's experience was typical for the absence from temporal reality reported by those who have had an "in-the-zone" event; the sense in retrospect of being displaced from the body. King told us she could not remember any significant details from her two-day Olympic trials performance.

"It was almost dreamlike," she said. "And, like a dream, the details became elusive and faded away."

King received a novocaine shot in her spine at the position of the healing vertebral disk to deaden the pain before she went through her Olympic trial paces. Surprisingly, the only discomfort she suffered from her physical activity was swollen Achilles tendons in both legs. By treating her legs with a heating salve and swathing them with bandages to trap the heat, then alternately applying ice to reduce the swelling, King was able to complete her performance with flying colors.

King observed that her experience of winning her pre-Olympic test after intense concentration for months on end, then passing through a dreamlike phase, was so deeply moving that it changed her life.

"I wanted to understand what in the hell happened to me. What had I done? I knew it was not possible to participate in athletics at the level I did without physical training. So I had accomplished the impossible. I started investigating and discovered a whole world of imagery, visualization and mental rehearsal — the same thing they are teaching astronauts and cancer patients and corporate executives. And I thought this was it — I had found it, like the Holy Grail. I got a grant, learned how to teach intense visualization, and thought that anyone who attended my lectures could take the powerful tool I taught and put it to work. But it wasn't effective that way.

"I went back to the drawing board and discovered something was missing. Of course, it was the passion that was missing. Without passion, there is no great arousal state. The great entrepreneurs, doctors, humanitarians, athletes, the movers and shakers, call on passion to excel. So, all I'm saying is that what I discovered is that exceptional human performance is a product of the alignment of passion, vision and action. It's what you guys call body, mind and spirit."

King said she wanted to make absolutely clear the personal motivation that permitted her to win her Olympic trials when she should not have been able to. She observed: "What any of us can actually accomplish depends on an energy source to fuel the effort. For example, people assume that it took a tremendous amount of willpower and discipline for me to achieve what I did on the Olympic level. While that may be true, I was never in touch with either willpower or discipline. What I did know every morning when I woke up was that there was nothing I wanted more on the face of this earth than to be an Olympian. You don't have to have willpower to get out of bed to do your favorite thing. You bound out of bed. The fuel for sustaining that kind of intensity, for feeling empowered and energized, is passion.

"Most people don't know what it feels like to call on this resource. A few people spend whole lifetimes operating at maximum capacity. The critical difference between them and people who achieve less, is passion. I'm sure that you, for example, have at some point in your life functioned or performed at a level far above usual. I'll bet you find those times of exceedingly high productivity were those when you were motivated by a feeling that came from very deep inside you. An ordinary person who taps into passion will access inner strength and hidden resources that she never knew she had. Passion allows you to focus on one specific goal and to pursue it all costs."

Passion was the inspiration that drove Stacy Allison to become the first American woman to climb Mount Everest, the highest mountain in the world. Raised in Portland, Oregon, with parents who encouraged her early to be competitive and to excel in swimming, Allison was astonished when, at age twelve, she lost her first race at the finals of a state swimming meet.

She quit swimming, she said, "because it was inconceivable to me that I would ever lose, and I wasn't prepared for it."

In retrospect, many years later when she returned to swimming for the fun of it, Allison resumed taking to the water for the sheer pleasure the sport gave to her. It was a lesson she would embrace as an adult who decided to challenge the world's highest mountain.

Allison's conviction that she would climb to the summit of the mightiest mountain — to be the first American woman to ascend to the shining snow-covered 29,028-foot tip came to her in 1982. That was the year she climbed Mount Washington, exalting in a sport which she had started in college. When she halted, exuberant and filled with enthusiasm on the flanks of Mount Washington near Seattle, she stopped in a moment of rest and took in the lofty vista of vaulting sky touching a descending dark green carpet of firs. That was the moment when she promised herself that she would be the first American woman to climb to the top of the world. She would stand at the peak of Everest, one of the few who ever reached the icy, windswept summit.

Her promise to herself was not arrogance, Allison said. "It was just something I knew. It was my vision, my passion. And it came to me on that day on Mount Washington with absolute clarity."

It was many years later before Allison realized fully what her pledge to herself that shining day on the mountain meant in terms of her personal journey through life. Without any question, the execution of her decision would give her proof of her excellence as a human, although she had not framed her promise to herself in such lofty language. She was certainly aware that the subject of her passion — the conquest of a mountain which had taken the lives of dozens who had tried to mount her peak — was certainly worthy of the extreme effort it would demand.

As it turned out, Allison climbed the mountain twice — once in 1987, when she didn't make it to the top, and again in 1988. But her reasons for both climbs were as different as the approaches to the roof of the world. Fresh from a divorce a year before her first climb, free from an abusive relationship, Allison said she saw the initial ascent as a sort of justification of herself, a statement to her former husband, to herself, to the world, that she was "somebody."

"When I made that climb," she said, "I was totally focused on the idea of proving who I was."

Her ascent in 1988 is the one which she wrote about in her book, *Beyond the Limits: A Woman's Triumph on Everest,* with Peter Carlin, and it was the trip that gave her the joyous, spirit-widening experience that makes of some mountain climbers, like Allison, people who have a deep connection to the mystery of the universe. That awesome mystery may have been at work in her favor in the early morning of September 28, 1988, when she and her team of climbers with insufficient bottled oxygen for all to complete the final assault on the peak, chose numbers to determine which climber would go all the way.

Allison won, and she started the final ascent, accompanied by a sturdy Sherpa, Pasang, who insisted his leathery lungs could draw enough oxygen out of the thin air to keep him going.

An excerpt from her book vividly tells the story of Allison's experience on the perfect day above the clouds:

" ... I sucked in a deep breath and reclaimed my courage. I've got to depend on myself. I started up the final stretch. A group of Korean climbers reached my position and joined me in the climb.

"The Hillary Step is the last major obstacle on the way to the summit. Mottled with natural ridges, gaps and pockmarks, the thirty-five-foot vertical cliff should be easy to climb.

"But at 29,000 feet, things look different. The cliffs loomed over an 8,000-foot drop, and I felt anxious. A lot of people make mistakes climbing easy walls. And now the wind was kicking up. Would it be strong enough to blow me off? A gust swept off my hat and sent it flying into Tibet. Luckily, I had a hood.

"I swung my ice ax and hoisted myself up, trying to shrug off my fear. Just another wall. Nothing special. It took about three minutes to climb to the top.

"Pasang looked up at me, hesitating. I waved him on, but he didn't move. Pasang, too, could feel the wind and emptiness beneath us. One slip on the ice and it's over.

"'It's okay!' I shouted. He visibly steeled himself, then began moving up the ice slowly, planting his ice ax, taking another step. I watched him climb for a few minutes, then turned for the summit.

"It was just seventy-five feet away! I'm so close. Something swelled inside me, but I pushed it down. I had to stay focused.

"Twenty-five feet. Adrenaline started surging into my fingers and even my dull toes. I'm going to make it.

"Ten feet. This was it. I checked my watch. Just past ten-thirty, September 29, 1988. I smiled behind my oxygen mask and took the last few steps. I was standing on top of the world.

"All of the tallest peaks below were covered by thick, billowing clouds. Up above, a few wispy clouds skimmed by the sun, riding the highest winds in the firmament. Pasang came up, pumping his ice ax in the air, hooting and yipping.

"A wave of emotion rose from my core. My eyes blurred behind my glasses. After months of controlling my thoughts, I could let it all go. That fragile dream I'd had so many years ago — and almost lost — had finally come true."

Allison said her motive for climbing Mount Everest in 1988 had a great deal to do with her success.

"When I didn't make it to the top in 1987, I had a lot of reassessing to do, and I had to look inside me. I realized that I don't climb to be first, I never have, and I never will again. And it didn't work for me. The reason I climb is for the joy and the challenge, physical and mental challenge, and the incredible environment. So what worked for me in 1988 was the fact that I wanted to go back to Everest, and I wanted to climb to the top of the mountain. I had a passion for the climb that had nothing to do with justifying me. It was something I had to do. It was a deeply personal, moving desire. Instead of trying to show somebody, as I had the previous year, my purpose for climbing the mountain was for myself. I knew I could make it to the top; I really believed in myself. It is very important to know why you're doing whatever it is you're doing. I wasn't looking over my shoulder that year at anyone else, and consequently I was a much better team player. I had a lot more energy to focus on the task at hand … on climbing."

Allison added the thought to her statement that places her and other outstanding achievers like Marilyn King in the company of passionate heroes: "For me what works is acknowledging the world around me and how I fit into all of that. When I'm climbing I feel I'm where I'm supposed to be. It is as if I'm not supposed to be down there working or doing something else. I feel truly that I belong when I'm climbing. It's where I feel most alive. It's my passion! It's where I feel most connected."

Of this connectedness, Alfred North Whitehead wrote, "Our minds are finite, and yet even in these circumstances of finitude, we are surrounded by possibilities that are infinite, and the purpose of human life is to grasp as much as we can out of that infinitude."

Don Schollander, the youth who, at eighteen, was voted the best athlete in the world, amateur or professional, told us unequivocally that no person who aspires to great things is going to accomplish them without a strong sense of passion for what he does.

"Passion is the right word. I think most people who are successful terrifically enjoy what they are doing, whether it's picking up garbage or competing in their sport, or whether it's the business they're in," Schollander said. "They have the passion for that activity and want to do it in the best way they possibly can. I know I wasn't always concerned about winning or losing. I had a passion for the sport, and my goal was to improve myself and get better every single time, but I didn't mind when I lost. That was the other side of me that helped a great deal. Because I was never disappointed. If I lost there was a reason, and I'd simply sit down and say to myself, 'Okay, now I'm going to learn something. When I win I don't learn anything.' Without passion, not only will you not be as happy as you can be, you won't be half as good as you can be. You have to have passion for whatever you are doing so that you don't necessarily care whether you are special or not; and then, and only then, you will be successful at what you've chosen to do."

Thinking back over his career, Schollander said, "I swam in the best of times — the great years of swimming. There were great competitors I swam against: Murray Rose from Australia, Roy Sarri and Steve Clark from the United States, Hans Klien from Germany, Bobby McGregor from Great Britain. All of us changed the sport of swimming; we were the pioneers of modern competitive swimming, and we had all the fun and excitement that goes with trail-blazing. There was certainly a spirit of passion that motivated each one of us."

The man who made the Swimming Hall of Fame when he was nineteen, won national championships and four Olympic gold medals, set thirty-seven American records and twenty-two world records, said that passion as a critical ingredient of success is typified by a statement he made in his book, *Deep Water:*

"In top competition a whole new ingredient enters swimming, one that you never know until you reach this level — pain. You learn the pain in practice and you know it in every race. As you approach the limit of your endurance it begins, coming on gradually, hitting your stomach first. Then your arms go heavy and your legs tighten — thighs first, then knees. You sink lower in the water because you can't hold yourself up; you are actually swimming deeper in the water as though someone were pushing down on your back. You experience perception changes. The sounds of the pool blend together and become a crashing roar in your ears. The water takes on a pinkish tinge. Your stomach feels as though it's going to fall out —

every kick hurts like hell — and then suddenly you hear a shrill, internal scream.

"In a race at the threshold of pain, you have a choice: you can back off — or you can force yourself to drive to the finish, knowing that this pain will become agony. It is right there at the pain barrier that the great competitors separate from the rest. Most swimmers back away from the pain; a champion pushes himself on into agony. Is it masochistic? In a way, yes. When it comes it is oddly satisfying because you know it had to come and now it is there because you are meeting it, taking it without backing down — because you enjoy the triumph of going through it knowing it is the only way you can win. It's those last few meters of the race, while you're in agony, that count. If you can push yourself through that pain barrier into real agony, you're a champion."

Pain, as Schollander acknowledged, and Stacy Allison and Marilyn King corroborated by their journeys of achievement, is part of the price of passion, a price with which champion auto racer Lyn St. James is all too familiar.

If rejection can be considered part of the pain of achieving championship status, St. James has had her share. In her twenty years of battling to carve out a career as a professional auto racer, she repeatedly has been told what she can't do, what she shouldn't attempt, and what she won't ever accomplish. Many times her own crew members, disdainful of her female pretensions in what they consider to be an all-male sport, have made it clear that she would be more welcome in the garage if she fetched coffee rather than ask questions about the chassis set-up of her racing car.

As she told us, "My entire career, it has always been, 'Who is going to work with a girl driver? Who is going to work with the bitch?' Many male drivers have told me, 'I couldn't put up with what you do.'"

Even St. James's mother — seventy-seven-year-old Maxine Cornwall, a strong woman who drove a cab in Painesville, Ohio, during World War II, has fought St. James's racing career because "it isn't ladylike." Mrs. Cornwall said in a *Sports Illustrated* interview, "My plan for Lyn was for her to get a good education and to be a nice lady. I didn't want her to be hard and fierce. She has wrinkles around her eyes. She has let herself go. Racing is her life. I say prayers for her, sometimes twice a day."

Despite objections from her mother, and the slights, jealousies and insults of men engaged in car racing, the turning point in St. James's journey came in 1991, when Ford Motor Company, her sponsor for ten years, drastically reduced its involvement in road racing and dropped her as a driver.

Forced to shop around for rides, St. James got only three races, so at the urging of friends she enrolled in a self-awareness seminar to help her come to grips with her sudden inactivity. After listening for two days to strangers make declarations about how they were going to change their lives, St. James announced, "I'm going to drive in the Indianapolis 500."

Speaking about the major force in her life, St. James said, "Why am I doing this? It comes down to passion. I love racing. I truly know that the gratification I get from driving is absolutely the most necessary thing in my life."

Almost anyone who knew Lyn St. James as Evelyn Cornwall, the introverted daughter of a Willoughby, Ohio, sheetmetal worker and his wife before she adopted St. James as her racing name, would have a hard time believing who she is today.

"I grew up," St. James said, "literally on the wrong side of the tracks." St. James said she led a sheltered life, didn't date much in high school, but did hang around with a group of public school kids who liked drag racing, and they began to bring her out of her shell. Of course, she discovered a strong interest in cars, and one night at a local drag strip she got up enough nerve to climb into one of the cars and race it. She still has her trophy for that race.

In 1963, Lyn's drag-racing friends decided to attend the Indianapolis 500. St. James begged her mother to allow her to go with them, and her mother gave her reluctant permission.

As she said to us, "The Indy 500 was the most incredible experience I've ever had. I was absolutely mesmerized by the whole thing. They wouldn't let me into gasoline alley [the pit and garage area] because women were not allowed there in those days. But I got to go to the drivers' meeting, which was open to the public. I saw A. J. Foyt and Mario Andretti. I never in a million years thought I'd be doing what they did. There just wasn't any point of reference for me. I was a girl. I loved that whole racing scene more than you could imagine, but there were no women racing there."

Twenty years later, St. James was driving on the same team with A. J. Foyt at Daytona.

Of her career and the passion that has made it soar, St. James said:

"Experiencing success and control in a race car has made me realize that I had capabilities and power as an individual — and not just all by myself, but as graded against other people of equal or greater strength. That has given me a sense of confidence I never had before. That is why I think auto racing is so special."

Today, Lyn St. James has put her name in the record books more than thirty-two times over her twenty-year racing career — most recently at the 1997 Indy 500.

The highlights of her career sparkle with accomplishments. She won the 1992 Indy 500 "Rookie of the Year" designation (only woman to ever win); she set the national closed course speed for women for the fifth time, reaching 225.7 miles per hour at the 1995 Indy 500 qualification. She qualified sixth at the 1994 Indy 500 (highest ever for a woman), and she set the record for the most starts by a woman, including her sixth-consecutive start at the Indy 500.

Throughout St. James's racing career, she has been recognized by numerous organizations and companies for her achievements and contributions. She continually strives to make a difference and to help pave the way for young girls and boys to participate in untraditional careers. Through the Lyn St. James Foundation, she has established programs that embrace this philosophy. St. James also is a past president and member of the Board of Stewards of the Women's Sports Foundation; an advisory board member of Human Performance International; chair of the advisory board of the Colorado Silver Bullets, the new all-female baseball team; consumer advisor and spokesperson for Ford Motor Company; director of consumer relations for the National Car Care Council; and spokesperson for the eighty-one automotive aftermarket parts stores of the Whitlock Corporation.

St. James told us that while passion has been the over-riding quality responsible for the personal drive which has placed her near the top of the auto racing world, she has relied on twelve important words — slogans actually — as keys to implementing her passion for success. She said she conferred with a sports psychologist to define the twelve-word foundation that supports her passion.

Following are the questions and answers we exchanged with St. James about her twelve slogans:

What are the twelve validating word-slogans in your life?

St. James: "The first one is 'right focus.' You have to be focused on the right thing. Everybody talks about being focused, but you have to be targeted on the right things, and the right things are those which are going to enable you to be at your championship level. In other words, focused means having your priorities really straight — seven days a week, whether I'm at the race track or not."

The next slogan, she said, is "common energy."

"By common energy I mean that everyone around you is energized with the same focus and holds the same priorities. Everybody on my team has to have that motivation. And my team means not only my race team, my family, my employees or the people I work with. This definition is the one that really forced me to describe the elements that are in place when I qualify at my best. By being able to describe yourself at your best, you will be able to reconstruct it and bring back the circumstances and feelings when you wish to."

The next slogan, St. James said, is "endurance."

"I have to be able to endure everything that's thrown at me. I've got to be able to outlast everybody in the sense of the race. Call it staying power if you wish. Often, people give up when they are closer than they know to winning."

The next slogan in St. James winning category are the words "physically strong."

"I have to be physically strong. Mentally I have to be strong. Strength works with endurance. You've got to have the strength to endure. That means you've got to take care of yourself."

"Leanness" is a St. James word.

"Leanness is very important," she said. "It is my focus every day, so that when I go out and spot such nice things as chocolate chip cookies, my leanness discipline kicks in, and I say no to the temptation. I fight this tooth-and-nail battle because I'm genetically not a lean person, but I know the person who is lean is going to have more endurance and more muscle strength."

"Alert thinking" is part of St. James's vocabulary.

"I have to be very alert to keep track of what's going on around me. And I have to keep the right focus to let go of things which are unimportant."

Lyn St. James uses the word "hungry" as almost a synonym for passion.

"It's like passion; it's the competitive desire to really want to have that best lap, that qualifying lap, that race lap, or to win the deal if you are in a business environment. I have to be hungrier than any body else."

St. James's last word, she said, is the one that is the toughest for her to define. She uses the word "selfing." We asked her what she meant by the word.

"It's a Lyn St. James word. A substitute for being selfish. To me, selfing means taking care of your personal needs. Whether it's a quiet moment you need or just making sure you do your exercise sessions when you should. Selfing also means honoring who you are, congratulating yourself for your achievements and having people around you who love you and whom you love to be associated with."

St. James observed that her twelve words were really a composite of the one word: "passion."

When St. James was named "Rookie of the Year" by *Auto Week* in 1984, it was proof that her slogans worked. But the victory she'll never forget is the historic one she won at Watkins Glen, New York, when she refused to get out of the car and let her co-driver finish the 500-kilometer race.

As she told an interviewer for the *Mercury Tracer,* "I wasn't tired, and I didn't need relief. So when I came into the pits to refuel, change tires and switch drivers, I just stared at my crew chief, Charlie Selix and didn't budge. My co-driver, Whitney Ganz, was standing there trying to help me get unstrapped, but I never looked at him, I just kept staring at Charlie, then I shook my head no. Charlie never flinched, and off I went."

As the magazine article explained, when Lyn got the checkered flag, the news media surrounded her. But she looked in vain for someone in her crew. They had been as sharp as ever during the latter stages of the race but didn't appear in the victory circle. Apparently, they were resentful of her decision to finish the race by herself. Later, Ganz took St. James aside and told her he would have done the same thing if he'd been in her shoes. He understood how she had been swept up in the passion of winning.

The "07" necklace St. James wears is dedicated to the number 07 Ford Probe, an 850-horsepower research vehicle in which she set the women's closed course speed record of 204.2 miles per hour. The record run took place at the Alabama International Motor Speedway in November 1985. There were times on the backstretch that day when Lyn hit 215 miles per hour.

"At that speed," she said, "you are driving the car at its absolute limits. Your visual reference points come up so much quicker. I felt like I was threading a needle. I wasn't frightened, but I can tell you it was eerie. At those speed levels, the car could just take over. That's where my own aggressiveness comes in."

In the final analysis, with all her ups and downs, St. James credits the vigor of her passion for racing as the single most important source of her personal power.

If unrelenting determination is the price of passion, then Mark Wellman, like Lyn St. James, proved that going after a goal with all your heart will overcome hardships, hurdles, and disappointments. This was certainly the case for Wellman, a paraplegic who became paralyzed from the waist down as the result of a hundred-foot fall while he was climbing a 13,700-foot peak south of Yosemite National Park in 1982.

After spending eight months in the hospital, Wellman got to thinking what he was going to do with his life and decided to go back to school, where he obtained a degree in park management. He became a ranger in Yosemite National Park.

"I remember," he said, "exactly my idea of being a park ranger. I was collecting three-dollar entry fees for admittance to the park and sucking in the auto fumes as cars drove in and out. This was after the accident." The next summer he was reassigned to the job as a park naturalist, and after that summer it turned into a permanent job with the National Park Service. It seemed inevitable, with his background of rock climbing, that he would become a rallying point for big-wall climbing at Yosemite Valley.

Not long after that he met Mike Corbett.

"I was wheelchairing out of my cabin one day, and I bumped into Corbett. I had a magazine called *Sports Spokes,* a wheelchair athletic magazine. On the front cover there was a picture of a woman being lowered down a cliff in a wheelchair. I showed it to Mike, and his eyes got real big. He knew who I was, and he said, 'Have you ever thought about rock climbing again?' I told him I had, but I knew my wheelchair was going to be a real hindrance on the rock. That was the beginning of an idea that turned into a twelve-day struggle up the sheer granite face of Yosemite's Half Dome."

Wellman said he and Corbett practiced for six months before climbing the most formidable unbroken granite cliff in North America.

"We really kind of pioneered what we were trying to do. I had to wear special pants that we dubbed "rock chaps" because I don't have feeling in my legs. It was real important that I protected my legs because basically I was pulling myself up a rope, dragging myself along the cliff, and if I ended up getting an abrasion sore on my leg, I could get an infection that could become a problem. So we really did our homework; we trained, we made sure the equipment was going to work right."

The grim battle for ascendance ended for the disabled climber and his partner when Wellman pulled himself onto the summit of Half Dome on a Sunday afternoon.

He and Corbett had climbed more than 300 feet Saturday, Wellman's most productive day of climbing since leaving the Yosemite Valley floor. The pair could see tourists and well-wishers waving to them at the summit about 200 feet above them.

"I'm looking forward to a hot bath, a hot meal and a cold beer," said Wellman by radio.

Between the climbers and the summit, though, had stood one of the most difficult and spectacular sections of the climb: a forty-foot overhang they had to attack directly.

Corbett was forced to drive pitons straight up into cracks in the overhang, a series of overlapping granite blocks that resembled the underside of a cantilevered bridge.

Wellman, using the mechanical ascenders with a pull-up bar, hung free on the rope in space, swinging like a windchime nearly a vertical mile above the valley floor. Friends of the climbers, support staff, and hundreds of curious tourists formed a line like an ant trail up the relatively easy east side of Half Dome. Supporters carried champagne and Pepsi to the top, and one person carried up Wellman's wheelchair so he could take a spin around Half Dome's expansive summit. By late Saturday, the wooded shoulder beneath the monolithic summit had become a bustling media village. Satellite dishes, radio antennas and cellular phones crackled in the pines.

Earlier, the climbers had been deluged by rough weather. The threat of snow at Half Dome's peak extended the expected weeklong climb. But Wellman remained cheerful, despite the delays, which included rain, wind and lightning. "We were expecting to be blown around last night but we weren't. That's kind of nice," Wellman said, adding, "It was scary."

In a reflective mood, Wellman said, "Time goes by fast from sunup to sundown up on the cliff surface. It goes real fast. Everything you do is a chore, whether you're eating, trying to pull food out of your haul bag, or you're trying to do upward mobility, like climbing. Everything is a lot of work and the time goes by very quickly. All of a sudden it's the next day, and as darkness starts to set in you need to set up your bed.

"Of course," Wellman said, "you're hanging on the cliff's face in your bed. When you're sleeping on a porta-ledge, you're finally not hanging from your waist anymore, but you're still tied into the rope. So for those of us who like to roll around at night, if you roll off the porta-ledge, the rope would catch you."

Mark said passion was the fire, the idea of pioneering an event no one else has done in quite the same way, that fueled the purpose of his climb up Half Dome. "The sea of granite, I like to call it. This is a huge monolith, and you don't realize how big it is until you're actually up there. You know, it's three times the size of the Empire State Building. That kind of gives you some idea. People down on the ground looking through binoculars at the climbers see them as insect-size. It's hard to fathom how huge this granite cliff is until you actually see a person up there through binoculars, and then you realize how insignificant he is. And yet, you have to admire the guts of the climber who pulls himself up, relying on his skill, his training and, when there's a real rough spot, his tenacity, the passion to go on, to not give up."

Sharing the company of passion-driven athletes like Marilyn King, Lyn St. James, and Mark Wellman, is Bonny Warner, who in 1980 as a torchbearer for the Winter Olympics, witnessed for the first time at Lake Placid, New York the dangerous practice of plunging down a tunnel of slick ice on a high-speed sled. She was captivated with the idea that she could become a champion in the sport of luging. By 1987, her determination had brought her a variety of medals and world cups in luging and ranking in the sport as number three in the world.

Warner said her opportunity to train for luging was a fluke. As a seventeen-year-old, she entered a lottery and won $5,000, which permitted her to go to Germany to train with the German national luge team, acknowledged then to be the best.

She admitted that her inspiration to train with the Germans was based on the suggestion given to her by a coaching friend, who really didn't expect a naive young American female to put his idea into action. But that's what Warner did. "Of course," Warner said, "the Germans must have thought I was something special, having flown all the way from the United States to be with them. They changed their minds the very first time I went down the course bent on killing myself."

Warner explained that her pell-mell descent on slick ice, mostly on her face, convinced the Germans that the reckless American needed caretaking or she was going to bash her brains out. "Either that or they figured by helping me they could get me off the track and send me home. Anyway, they decided to help the American kid. They adopted me and started coaching me on the basics and the fine points of luging."

The German team's admiration for the determination — the passion — of the American, her absolute dedication to learn the luging sport, was no doubt justified in their minds by the incredible number of crashes Warner made. Forty-one times the American went flying down the treacherous icy path on steel runners and was thrown into bruising contact with the thick, icy walls before she made a "clean" run by staying on her sled. Warner explained that the design of luge sleds in those days did not protect the driver's arms.

Imagine flying off a whizzing steel sled traveling at speeds up to seventy miles per hour and smashing onto a solid wall of ice with your arms taking the brunt of the punishment! But this was the grueling routine to which Warner subjected herself, learning slowly to balance properly on the luge; learning the secrets of steerage, body positioning, and weight distribution. Thinking back on her apprenticeship, Warner said, "Yes, it was a lot of punish-ment, but you don't think about that when you are caught up in your passion. Every time I fell off, bounced against those solid walls, I learned. I know, some people think to go through such torture is crazy. Maybe it is, but if it's what you've got to do, you pay the price. It may hurt, but it's worth it to emerge as a champion, to know you are the best there is."

So bruised and battered did Warner become that she had to stop luging for a week. During that time, she iced her flesh to reduce the swelling. Her arms, her whole body, had been pummeled so badly that her skin in places was stretched as tight and shiny as a drum.

Unable to afford proper arm pads, Warner discovered a bundle of tourist brochures and, with duct tape, stuck them together to make padded sleeves, which she wore as protective lining between her insulating long underwear and her coat. Her kind of devotion to perfection personifies how passion creates champions.

Warner has taken her winning attitude to the United States Olympic Committee, where she has served on the Athletes' Advisory Committee. There, like Lyn St. James, Don Schollander, Stacy Allison and others, she passes on to aspiring athletes the flame of passion, "... the fever of the mind" that leads to high accomplishment and validation of the self.

7

Building the Will to Win Through Motivation

Ultimately, no one else "does it for us" or "does it to us;" the status we reach in life is totally our own doing, a consequence of our thoughts and actions, our motivation. To take responsibility for our outcomes, we need to recognize the Giant Killers and Self-Actualizers that either hinder us or bolster us. It is the absence of an essential actualizer, or the presence of a debilitating killer, that undermines our motivation, our accomplishments, and therefore our lives. Great coaches are first good motivators, and they motivate by using the actualizers and avoiding the killers listed in this chapter. The best coach you can ever have is yourself and, like other great coaches, you have to apply the motivational tool chest outlined in this chapter.

In Chapter Six we quoted William Penn, who wrote that, "Passion is a sort of fever in the mind." Taking the next step of associating passion to motivation we arrive at the inescapable conclusion that how an athlete, or any person, achieves success is dependent unquestionably and entirely on how he thinks.

This has proved to be true of the men and women we've interviewed. They have showed us that when an athlete breaks through barriers, he demonstrates the power of the mind to free the individual to do what are considered to be impossible things.

If we could but convince ourselves of the power that lies within each one of us, and if we could suspend our doubts about the physical impact on us of something so fundamental as the words we speak to ourselves and others, then we would discover there is nothing we wish to achieve that is beyond our reach. This idea was presented twenty years ago by the famous physiologist Sir John Eccles when he proposed in his book, *Research in Parapsychology,* that the simple act of saying a word is actually a form of psychokinesis: "The mind has been able to work upon the brain cells, just slightly changing them....The mind is making these very slight and subtle changes for hundreds of millions of cells, gradually bringing [the word or words] through and channeling it into the correct target cells to make the movement. And so there is psychokinesis (PK), mind acting upon a material object, namely, brain cells. It's extremely weak, but it's effective because we've learned to use it."

Posing a question on how Eccles' thought might be actually applied by an athlete, *In the Zone* authors Murphy and White asked:

"What if an athlete can control his muscles the same way that a PK subject in the laboratory can control the throw of a die? If mind is the prime mover, then the muscles are just as much 'outside' the mind as the die face or the table lamp that Johnny Muller said we will one day move by mind alone. Or, put the other way, the die face or lamp are no more outside the reach of the mind than one's muscles. The sports literature suggests that a few individuals who are able to perform extraordinary feats view reality in this way. Baseball enthusiast Richard Grossinger observed: 'Pitchers have torn muscles, broken bones, been operated on, had ligaments grafted; they have altered everything about their delivery and rhythm that made them a pitcher in the first place. They have come back from rotary cuff surgery, from not being able to lift their arms for a year and a half, and they have won ballgames.' "

"Physical handicaps, too," Murphy and White said, "can be transcended. Kitty O'Neil lost her hearing at age four, but she became a champion diver, set the world's record as the fastest woman water-skier, became an expert in motorcycle racing, and then became a stuntperson in movies, setting two records for women: a 112-foot fall and the highest fall while on fire ever attempted.

She told Phil Bowie that she was motivated by a liking for danger and thrills, but added: 'Mostly I want always to have a goal, some dream that I can try for.'" It's obvious by her performance and her statement that O'Neil, like dozens of other athletes and highly motivated persons, considered it inconceivable not to believe that her mental state, her attitude, had more to do with her accomplishment than her body. Her body was the tool that transmitted her intentions, acted on her motivation.

We believe, and will demonstrate, that there is one axiom, one universal truth that is the basic principle of all human performance teaching:

Whatever prevails in your mind will manifest in your world.

You have heard this message phrased in different ways: "You will become whatever you think about most."

"As a man thinketh in his heart, so he becometh."

"The universe will return to you the value of your thoughts."

Once you understand the power of this concept — and this chapter is devoted to bringing this power to you — you will be able to alter not only the physical shape and function of your body, but your attitudes and mental efficiency, your way of being in the world. You will immediately begin to experience a kinder, more fulfilling existence. So true and effective is this message that the great spiritual leaders throughout the centuries have preached its history-altering power. Mahatma Gandhi was able to use it to convince millions of his countrymen that if they would replace violence in their minds with thoughts of self-autonomy they would find a peaceful transition to self-rule.

If it is true that you become and receive what you think about most, then it follows that the only discipline you need in life is control over what you think about. If you change the manner in which you think and what you think about, inescapably you will change your life. Stop for a moment! Stop as you consider this statement and apply it to yourself and prevent yourself from listening to your inner voice of doubt, the one that preaches justification of failure, the one that permits you to excuse yourself from any challenge to your complacency.

We are challenging you to override your veto voice, and put absolute trust in the statement: The only discipline you need in life is control over what you think about. If you can do this, we promise that you will have the key to winning the goal in your life of which you may have only dared to dream.

All of us give ourselves reasons not to make a dream come true. They take form as:

I am not worthy.

I am not smart enough.

I am too thin.

I am too fat.

I don't have enough education.

I'm overqualified.

I'm too old.

I'm too young.

The list of excuses is endless; you have your own with which you have limited your performance. One thing is absolutely certain: If you listen to your veto voice, it will convince you of your inability to accomplish what is secretly dear to your heart.

We are going to investigate the veto voice in this chapter, how and why it rises to fill you with doubts, and we will show you how to overcome and silence it. But first let's look at a man who, at five-foot-three-inches, a stunted sprout among towering oaks on the playing courts, is absolutely unqualified to be a star basketball player, yet has been voted Most Valuable Player by his team, and earns more than $2 million per year doing what he is incapable of doing.

Before you meet Muggsy Bogues, see if you can identify yourself or someone you know in this scene that describes a mother, father, and a child having a meal in a restaurant.

A family of three are traveling to visit with relatives and have stopped for breakfast at a diner in Maryland before continuing on south. The father notices that his eight-year-old son has pushed away his orange juice.

"Drink your juice," he orders.

Dismayed, the boy answers, "But I hate orange juice."

"Never mind what you like or don't like. Drink it. It's good for you."

"Aw, but Dad, I really don't want it," the boy says, appealing to his mother for support.

She chimes in and says, "Harvey, why make the boy drink something he dislikes so intensely?"

"Why?" the father answers with a stern, aggrieved expression on his face. "Because, just like me, he's got to learn. All my life I've done things I hate to do."

A version of this story was written by the philosopher Joseph Campbell. The point is, this unhappy father demonstrated his futility and repressed anger with himself by forcing his son to knuckle under to the rule of negativity that had governed the parent's life. The strong veto voice in the father's experience ruled his expectations of himself and dampened his aspirations. A bitter man, he saw his son's small rebellion as a mistake that must be corrected for his own good. Without understanding the extent of his influence, he was conditioning his son to view life in the same limited fashion as his parent.

If not for his attitude, his "I'm going to rise above my difficulties" spirit, Muggsy Bogues — like champion fencer Peter Westbrook, and world champion wrestler Chris Campbell — may have become another crime statistic from the dangerous neighborhood in which he grew up.

A story in *The New York Times* described how Bogues, the shortest basketball player in NBA history, "grew up in the tough Lafayette housing projects of Baltimore, where he once saw a man beaten to death with a baseball bat, another stabbed repeatedly with an icepick, where gunshots regularly rang out, where he himself was shot in the arm and back when he was five, where he wouldn't take the elevator in his building because he never knew who might have trapped him there. He walked up the ten flights of stairs instead to the family's modest apartment."

Bogues avoided drugs and crime and gangs, the choice of many to find big money and even some stature in the neighborhood. "All it would take was about two seconds to get in trouble, or get killed," Bogues said. He avoided trouble for several reasons, one of them being that his father, Richard, had been sentenced to prison for twenty years for armed robbery, had also been a drug dealer and addict, and was a model for Bogues in what not to do.

According to *The New York Times* story, Muggsy had great ambivalence about his father — as he does about his old neighborhood — and he eventually became friends with his father, visiting him in prison and corresponding with him when he was in college. But it was his mother, Elaine, who held the family together, Muggsy recalled. It was his mother who ruled Muggsy and his two older brothers and sisters. Elaine went on welfare when her husband went to prison, but decided that she could not continue in that fashion and made herself earn a high school equivalency diploma at night while working as a secretary in nonprofit organizations. She was able to put food on the table and clothes on her kids' backs, Muggsy said.

"My mom always brought home a present once a week for all of us. We never felt like we ever needed anything. We never felt poor. So I never felt I had to go out and do something wrong to get money." And it was his mother who consoled him when he came home crying that he wanted to be taller.

"You'll do fine, Ty," she said gently. "God doesn't make mistakes."

It was inevitable that Muggsy's determination would take him through college and into the world of basketball despite the fact that his height should have made him ineligible.

As unfolded in *The New York Times* story, Bogues became the most valuable player in the recreational leagues and graduated from that status to the most valuable player on his undefeated high school team in 1983; it was chosen number one in the nation. From there he became the most valuable player at Wake Forest, the college he attended. He was the Washington Bullets' first-round draft pick, but was given little playing time, and, as he recalled, suffered a loss of confidence for one of the first times in his basketball life.

As *The New York Times* story said: "Don't worry, you'll get your chance — you'll make it," Moses Malone, a teammate, told Bogues often. How was it that a seven-foot player could be so encouraging? "Because he was knowledgeable about basketball," Bogues said. And, of course, Bogues did make it. He has now become one of the most popular athletes with the Charlotte Hornets. His easy smile is a part of the landscape. Bogues is also a popular figure with advertisers on a national level, including a soft-drink commercial called "Muggsy vs. Goliath."

He sees himself as a possible inspiration to others — some may call it a role model — and is content to fit that mold.

"I'm a living example of not giving up," Muggsy said, a statement that described the deep competitive motivation that has made him a champion.

Watching Muggsy Bogues on the playing court gives a spectator a clear viewpoint of why he's such a valuable player. The "runt" is like a pest, buzzing in and out, stealing the ball from beanpole players, scooting — some fans have sworn — under and through the spread legs of opponents; shooting accurate speedball baskets through glimpsed holes made by taller moving bodies. Far from bewailing his stunted height, Bogues has made an asset of it.

The determination and positive frame of mind displayed by Bogues is a strong example of why it is true that what you get in life is more dependent upon your prevailing thoughts than any other influence.

Now, let's examine why this is so:

By understanding how the major components of the mind work, it will be easier for you to comprehend why what you receive in life is more dependent upon your prevailing thoughts than any other single influence. Muggsy Bogues has certainly demonstrated that this is true.

First let's divide the mind into three principal parts: the conscious, the self-conscious, and the subconscious. This three-tier division is widely accepted among psychology professionals, but here, we believe, we have presented a provocative and empowering way of interpreting the interactions of these three mental components.

Our interpretation is a blend of Eastern and Western thought. Pragmatic Westerners, largely driven by a mechanistic view of the world, see the brain as a machine, while Easterners seek to discover what is the best way to use the apparent powers of the mind.

It is Larry Dossey, philosopher/physician, who describes the conflict between those who insist on restricting the mind to supervision of the body and others who believe in the non-local nature of the mind. In his book, *Recovering the Soul,* he makes this intriguing statement:

"'Mind,' 'soul,' and 'consciousness'... what do these different words mean? Alas, it is not possible to separate these concepts in a universally acceptable way. Biologists, information theorists, artificial intelligence experts, and other scientists take many different positions, which usually conflict with those of philosophers, psychologists, and theologians. And the differences are not trivial. For some, 'mind' simply does not exist. It is a 'ghost in the machine,' a redundant and unnecessary abstraction of events that can be fully explained in uninflated, physical terms. For others, 'mind' is a 'category mistake,' a 'confusion of explanatory levels,' or an epiphenomenon or byproduct of chemical actions within the brain. Still others regard it as an entity that is quite real."

But Dossey points out that there "… is a greater reason to explore the non-local nature of the mind than simply to 'be accurate' [about the location of the mind] in some logical or scientific sense." This reason, he said, is conveyed by the Nobel neurophysiologist Sir John Eccles:

"Man has lost his way ideologically in this age … science has gone too far in breaking down man's belief in his spiritual greatness … and has given him the belief that he is merely an insignificant animal that has arisen by chance and necessity in an insignificant planet lost in the great cosmic immensity…. We must realize the great unknowns in the material makeup and operation of our brains and in the relationship of the brain to the mind and in our creative imagination."

"The main reason," says Dossey, "to establish the non-local nature of the mind is, then, spiritual. Local theories of the mind are not only incomplete, they are destructive. They create the illusion of death and aloneness, altogether local concepts. They foster existential oppression and hopelessness by giving us an utterly false idea of our basic nature, advising us that we are contracted, limited, and mortal creatures locked inside our bodies and drifting inex-orably toward the end of time. This local scenario is ghastly, and it is regrettable that it continues to dominate the picture put forward by most of our best psychologists and biochemists."

Dossey says he tries to show why this is a false view. His point is that if it is false and we are non-local instead of local creatures, then the world changes for us in the most glorious ways. For if the mind is non-local, it must in some sense be independent of the strictly local brain and body. This opens up the possibility, at least, for some measure of freedom of the will, since the mind could escape the deter-minative constraints of the physical laws governing the physical body. And if the brain is non-local, unconfined to brains and bodies, and thus not entirely dependent on the physical organism, the possibility for survival of bodily death is open. Then there is the nature of our relationship to each other. If the mind is non-local in space and time, our interaction with each other seems a foregone conclusion. "Non-local minds," he says, "are merging minds, since they are not 'things' that can be walled off and confined to moments in time or point-positions in space."

"If non-local mind is a reality," Dossey concludes, "the world becomes a place of interaction and connection, not one of isolation and disjunction. And if humanity really believed that non-local mind was real, an entirely new foun-dation for ethical and moral behavior would enter, which would hold at least the possibility of a radical departure from the insane ways human beings and nation-states have chronically behaved toward each other. And, further, the entire existential premise of human life might shift toward the moral and the ethical, toward the spiritual and the holy. Non-local mind potentially leads, to borrow historian and sociologist Morris Berman's provocative phrase, 'to a re-enchantment of the world.'"

But here we are talking about re-enchantment of the individual, and this can happen when you understand how the mind, which we prefer to believe is non-local, operates to develop, enhance or disparage imagination and ideas for action based on creative thought processes.

So, we will begin our approach to the mind with the Western orientation and describe the three major operating functions of the mind. Mind should be distinguished from brain because mind incorporates the relationship with the total organism, whereas the brain is a computer mass in the center of the head.

The three chief components of the mind, as we stated earlier, are the conscious, the subconscious, and the self-conscious. We prefer to substitute the word self-image for self-conscious. We will briefly describe these components and then show how they can work in unison to concentrate the true power we possess on the outcomes we desire.

The Conscious

The conscious controls overt behavior. It gathers information needed for decision making from five of the seven senses: sight, smell, hearing, taste, and touch. (The other two senses, creative intelligence and intuition, arise from within the brain.) The conscious mind makes routine decisions such as whether you should jump over a log, step up on it and then over it, or find a path around it. It determines whether you should offer a cheery good morning to your boss or if you should quickly get behind your desk and test his or her mood later. By using information stored in the subconscious and the self-image's impression of personal capability, your conscious mind makes the analytical decisions necessary to move you through a day's activities.

The most life-determining function of the conscious mind is to decide that which you will focus upon. It channels your thoughts on what it believes is most important and, by channeling your focus, it is the course-finder that determines where you will go in life. Its power lies in its ability to determine direction, not in its processing capability. Neurobiologists estimate that the conscious mind putters along doing three to five calculations per second, with spurts to forty calculations per second for individuals with the most developed conscious minds, such as football quarterbacks and concert pianists. This calculating power is scant compared to the subconscious, which can record data — but not make decisions — at the rate of one million information bits per second.

Although it has only a limited computing power, the conscious mind has ample power to formulate your thoughts. From external input, such as the coach who tells you that you are a lousy three-point shooter, or parents who inform you that "no one in our family can write well," to an experience in which you fail because you weren't properly prepared, the conscious mind develops thoughts and sends them to the subconscious.

The Subconscious

Herein lies the vast power of the mind. The subconscious exists only to accomplish what the conscious mind is focusing upon. As an indication of the power of the subconscious, remember that chess great Gary Kasporov was able to defeat a linkup of sixteen sophisticated computers in a competition. The computers were analyzing two million outcomes per second with no chance of error. Yet, Kasporov defeated them. When you focus on a goal, the mind can outperform any level of computing power to make your goal come true.

The power of the subconscious seems unrealistic until you realize the vast information that is readily available to it — all of the ideas, impressions, memories, actions, dreams — everything you've ever seen, experienced, witnessed or imagined (your human history) — are recorded in the subconscious. The subconscious maintains two data banks; one contains memories of all the significant and insignificant events in your life; the other contains all the knowledge you have acquired. Those forgotten history dates are still stored in the recesses of your mind. Also, it is your subconscious that maintains a two-way information flow with all the systems of the physiological body. When something isn't right, whether it is the beginning of a tumor or a foreign virus entering your body, the subconscious knows how to immediately send immune system cells to fight the invasion.

Larry Dossey tells a story about a middle-aged woman which demonstrates the remarkable power of the subconscious:

Elizabeth had been suffering from a pain in the lower left side of her abdomen. Having practiced meditation for years, she decided to center her mind and discover what information about her pain might come up to her consciousness.

Placing herself into a relaxed state, she stilled her conscious mind and waited tranquilly. What appeared eventually as a picture in her mind was a spherical-shaped form with three white spots on it. She knew that it was part of her body, probably one of her ovaries, about which her gynecologist had been concerned.

When she came out of her meditation, Elizabeth was relieved to know in her heart that she did not have cancer, but decided to visit her internist who was Larry Dossey.

Dossey, unlike many physicians who arrogantly deprecate self-diagnosis, listened to Elizabeth explain her version of the organ with the three white spots. Her self-assurance impressed him, and together he and she decided she would have a pelvic examination and a sonogram.

Dossey warned the radiologist who would supervise the sonogram that Elizabeth had predicted a picture of her ovary which showed the three white spots which she was sure were benign. Rolling his eyes, the radiologist said, "Oh, sure. We've heard that before, haven't we?"

Dossey explained what happened next in his book, *Recovering the Soul:*

"I went back to my office, only to be interrupted a half-hour later in a conversation with a new patient by a loud knock on my door. Excusing myself, I rose to answer it. It was the radiologist, and he was obviously upset. He was gesticulating in uncharacteristic fashion and was speaking so fast I could hardly understand him. I stepped into the hall for privacy, closing my office door behind.

"Jim, not so fast. I can't understand a word you're saying. What's bothering you?"

"That woman's crazy!" he stammered. I'd never seen him so off-balance.

"Never mind the psychiatric diagnosis, Jim. What did the sonogram show?"

Still angry, still fuming about his encounter with Elizabeth, Jim struggled to find the words.

"Three little white spots, just like she said! That's what she's got, all right. Three cystic lesions which look precisely like small white areas, benign-appearing, and all on the left ovary, the right ovary normal, and no sign of cancer anywhere! Damn it, how the hell did she know?"

"Well, Jim, with diagnostic skills like that, she could obviously put us both out of business."

"Elizabeth's pain continued in the days that followed. I referred her for a second opinion to another gynecologist, a female physician cordial to her views. They developed a warm relationship. Eventually Elizabeth grew weary of the pain, and both she and her gynecologist agreed that surgery seemed indicated. The operation, like the sonogram, confirmed Elizabeth's diagnostic acumen: on the left ovary were three completely benign cysts. Following surgery, which was uneventful, her pain disappeared completely and she remains well."

As Dossey pointed out, the radiologist's automatic disbelief rejection is typical of many people who encounter the enormous capacities of the mind for the first time in medical situations. Everyone "knows" that the mind can only do so much. It is lodged in the brain, a passive receptor and processor of sensory data, dependent on the brain's anatomy and physiology, a byproduct of biochemical reactions that occur in brain tissue which, if destroyed, causes the destruction of the mind as well.

Dossey further observed, however, that prejudices about how the mind should function don't fit with the clinical reality of how it does function, as an enormous body of evidence in medicine attests. Apparently, in Elizabeth's case, the mind never got the message about how it ought to behave.

"If cases like Elizabeth's were rare, perhaps they would deserve no more than a raised eyebrow. But they aren't. Medicine is thickly littered with similar examples showing that the mind's range is beyond the brain," Dossey said.

There are two more functional components of the subconscious. The first maintains the patterns — habits and attitudes — that make up your personality. The second, which we call the ideal self, is the seat of your intuition. There are certain things which a healthy, uncluttered mind is able to extract from all the input it receives, a sort of synthesis of feeling that can be trusted. Within our ideal self is stored the basic realization that we are pre-programmed to choose right over wrong. The ideal self houses the information which tells us that loving our neighbor takes us to a higher destiny than hurting our neighbor does.

Although the subconscious does not make decisions, it can make discoveries. Surely you have experienced moments when the light suddenly went on and the solution to a perplexing problem just popped into your head. This was your subconscious discovering an association between stored information and new information, the unity of the two important to the solution of a problem/challenge upon which the conscious was dwelling.

The Self-Image

The third component of the mind is called the self-image. The self-image reflects your beliefs about yourself and the world. The self-image is primarily a filter between the conscious and subconscious. As information comes in from the conscious mind, the self-image screens it and asks,

"Is this consistent with information already stored in the subconscious and consistent with how I, the self-image, see myself?" If yes, the information passes through; and if not, it is either rejected or altered to fit the existing beliefs. This phenomenon of altering data is apparent all around us. Two people can witness the same accident and see two entirely different "sets of facts." Witnesses seldom agree about who started a fight. What you see depends on which combatant is your friend and what you believe about your friend.

From this mind-editing function several incredibly powerful realizations become apparent: If you wish to change who you are, then you have to change either the input your conscious mind receives, i.e., change your environment (which can be a very successful strategy), or you have to change the manner in which your mind filters information. Those are the two options for personal growth. (It is true, however, that hypnosis can bypass both the conscious and the self-image to alter the makeup of the subconscious.)

Eva Auchinclos, founder of the Women's Sports Foundation, knows what it is to create change in the self and to teach it to female athletes who, like their male counterparts, often don't know where to go with their lives when they are no longer able to compete.

If ever anyone could change herself for the better, it is Eva Auchinclos, a pivotal force behind the success of women's sports in America. She is the woman who showed up eleven years ago when the fledgling Women's Sports Foundation was in its infancy and needed someone to make it grow. She gladly took charge, creating a national network from a bankroll of only $500.

Eva was used to taking charge. A native of Wayzata, Minnesota, who got married shortly after graduating from

Vassar College, she claims never to have been "an ordinary housewife" despite years of child raising and homemaking in an affluent New Jersey suburb. She was an active community organizer and the first woman to run for a seat on the local township committee.

Then her husband died and, later, after remarrying and moving to California, Eva landed a job as associate publisher at *Women's Sports*. Here her responsibilities were circulation, particularly newsstand sales, public relations, and "keeping peace between editorial and advertising."

When the magazine moved to New York the next year, Eva decided to stay behind, determined to make the Women's Sports Foundation work. It wasn't easy at first. "We were constantly applying for grants, and we never got any money," she recalled. "It was hard to get people to understand that women's sports was as worthy a cause as cancer research."

Eva learned quickly that her best resources were the well-known female athletes, such as Billie Jean King, Wyomia Tyus, and Sheila Young Ochowicz. She planned auctions, awards ceremonies, and gala banquets to showcase star athletes. "We learned to trade on the glitz to get money." It was not the glitz, however, that carried Eva through ten years of ups and downs at the helm of the foundation. It was a strong belief that childhood participation in sports leads to the development of successful women.

"Play and sport are primarily socializing factors," she said. "Perfecting sports skills is not as important as learning to compete and be a team player; learning to be responsible for yourself. Learning to change yourself to be the person you would like to be," Eva said.

Eva said her upbringing provided her with a basis for the changes she was able to make in her own life. "The truth is, I had three brothers and I was brought up in a male atmosphere. I played hockey and football ... you're handicapped in business and many other endeavors if you haven't learned to socialize in the same way as boys. The initial purpose of the foundation was to alter women's self-image by giving them the environment — sports — to see themselves as capable and strong."

Those who know Eva well draw a close link between the quality she brought to her job and the success of the Women's Sports Foundation.

"Women should be proud," she said, "to become the best that they can be. Competing in sports gives a woman a strong sense of herself, which is important for career modeling and business after sports."

By now, with examples such as Eva Auchinclos, it should be clear that conscious, subconscious and self-image constitute the hardware of the mind, but in order for them to interface they need operating software. The software that integrates the three frequently is called the reticular activating system. You don't have control over the RAS; it silently functions to create what your conscious mind is focused on. If your desire is to become the ultimate you, however you define this, then the RAS synchronizes the three hardware components to achieve this state.

Through experiences you have had the amazing ability of the RAS can be demonstrated. If you own a red Ford Taurus, you may discover how surprising it is how many other Ford Tauruses you're able to notice. Walk through a crowded parking lot and in the corner of your peripheral vision you may spot a car just like yours. If you're a coin collector, an old-looking penny in a tray of dozens jumps out at you. If you're driving down the road at sixty-five miles per hour and you believe round objects are dangerous, a ball-shaped rock on the verge of the road will attract your attention. This facility is the RAS at work; your senses see all and report all to the subconscious. The RAS coordinates conscious and subconscious mind to report anything of significance. That one small ball-shaped rock, if it is significant, will be red-flagged by the subconscious, and a cautionary warning relayed back to the conscious so that it can take proper action — avoidance, curiosity, or whatever is appropriate. After you have identified what is important to you, the RAS will automatically alert you to opportunities to fulfill your goals.

One of the powerful principles available for human development is the knowledge that positive experiences can be stored directly in the memory information bank, not only experiences that happen to the individual, but also those that are vividly imagined. Through the proper use of your imagination, you can transport a message directly to the subconscious. This is the whole principle behind the mental performance tool called visualization. This information is extremely useful because it makes possible — by altering the subconscious — important growth changes an individual may wish to make. The Workshop of the Mind we discussed earlier is an example of visualization. Therefore, self-image, goals, and values can be transformed. Knowing that you have this ability makes confidence-building and the process of self-motivation easier, although there are deliberate techniques involved in reaching the subconscious. One of these is called "centering," a subject to which the chapter entitled "Inward Bound with Alexander Everett" is largely devoted. Centering means going inside to the center of the self to create balance, inspiration, and power through contact with the spirit within. Centering benefits have been compared to the efficacy of prayer and, in a very real sense, centering and prayer are similar in that they can produce an altered state, both in the "actualizer" and the "receiver" of the intention of the prayer or the centering.

An example of direct intention, of how prayer can affect people, was demonstrated in a controlled experiment by Randolph Byrd, formerly a University of California professor, who designed a ten-month computer study to determine if prayer would benefit 192 coronary care unit patients. In the controlled experiment at San Francisco General Hospital of 393 persons, 201 were excluded from the prayer messages of home prayer groups directed at the designated patients. The results were amazing. The benefits for the prayed-for patients proved that:

They were five times less likely than the unprayed-for patients to require antibiotics, and they were three times less likely to develop pulmonary edema. Fewer of the prayed-for group expired during the experiment than patients in the other group, and none of the prayed-for group required endotracheal intubation, while twelve in the unprayed-for group required mechanical ventilatory support.

According to observers who studied the data from the experiment, if the technique being studied had been a new drug or a surgical procedure instead of prayer, it would almost certainly have been heralded as some sort of significant "breakthrough." Even so, anyone can appreciate the striking implications of this study. Even hard-boiled skeptics seem to agree on the significance of Byrd's findings. Dr. William Nolan, who has written a book debunking faith healing, acknowledged, "It sounds like this study will stand up to scrutiny ... maybe we doctors ought to be writing on our order sheets, 'pray three times a day.' If it works, it works."

What lessons does this study hold for us in our search to understand the mind and its role in medicine and in the many cases of mind influencing matter? The implications are far-reaching and take us into spiritual considerations. But for now, we can emphasize some of the non-spiritual aspects of prayer that shed important light on the nature of the mind. The San Francisco General Hospital study suggests that something about the mind allows it to intervene in the course of distant happenings (psychokinesis), such as the clinical course of patients in a coronary care unit hundreds or thousands of miles away. It was evident in this prayer study that the degree of spatial separation (distance) did not seem to matter. According to evaluators of the study, Byrd discovered that prayer groups which were located hundreds of miles away from the hospital were equally as effective as those which were situated just around the corner.

If motivation through centering, self-taught meditation, prayer, the Workshop of the Mind, affirmations, are the energizing force for control of purposeful behavior toward specific goals, then the reverse, negative thoughts, feelings of inferiority, directionless behavior, are the killers of a positive self-image.

8

Giant Killers and Self-Actualizers

───

Most of us do not realize the extent to which we are influenced by the way we think.

As we explain in Chapter Eight, Giant Killers are negative statements about yourself. Since you are your own most believable authority on yourself, the Giant Killers you introduce into your life become strong negative elements which can destroy your dreams, short-circuit your goals, and sabotage your objectives.

In this chapter we discuss how to overcome Giant Killers, turning them into self-actualizers that work for you instead of against you.

Nothing undermines success more than making negative statements about yourself. We call them giant killers. Do any of the following declarations resemble words which have slipped from your mouth?

1. Writing is really difficult for me.
2. Everything I eat goes right to my hips.
3. There is nothing I can do about it. Women don't find me attractive.
4. I'll never understand my teenage daughter.
5. It just isn't in the cards for me to be rich.
6. I'm too short to play basketball.

By applying what we know about how the mind works you can see why negative statements like those above become self-fulfilling prophecies. Let's analyze how your mind reacts to the first negative. The conscious mind, for whatever reason — it doesn't matter — confirms that you hate writing. If this statement has been affirmed before, the reaffirmation goes to your filter, your self-image, which says, "Yep, that's me. I sure do hate to write," and it sends the information on to the subconscious. The subconscious, which recognizes this negative from viewing it before, has an expedient filing system for it and creates a larger data base, reconfirming what it interprets as a "fact." Remember, all information that gets to the subconscious is true as far as it is concerned. As you add self-defeating information to negative data already recorded in the subconscious, you are piling more stones on a mountain of denial. Reversing negative information is difficult because often the denial you have built is sturdy and resists change.

An example of building a small mountain of denial was discovered by Lyle Nelson while he was having lunch at the Olympic Training Center in Lake Placid, New York. He said to his teammate, John Ruger, "I always miss my fifth shot in the standing position."

He was referring to the requirement in the biathlon for competitors to ski into the shooting range and fire five shots lying down, then ski another loop and again fire five shots from the standing position. Ruger, the oldest member of the team, displayed the fact that he was probably the wisest when he said to Nelson, "Lyle, you always will."

With just four words, Ruger made Nelson deeply aware of the damage his self-talk was doing to his overall performance. During Nelson's last Olympics, he shot clean standing (hit all the targets) in both of his races, a performance resulting from changing his self-talk and never repeating his negative statement concerning his fifth shot. As discussed, Giant Killer Number One is negative self-talk.

Giant Killer Number Two is worrying about things unlikely to happen or which are completely out of your control.

You can be sure your worst fears will certainly come to pass if you dwell on them, for the body manifests what the mind harbors. It should be readily apparent by now that the subconscious does not make distinctions between "good" or "bad" information. It can't discern whether or not the messages it receives are in the best interest of the individual. It relies on the conscious mind to make that determination. This is an important fact to remember. To achieve what you wish, you must monitor the language you use to get to your goals. If you are riddled with doubts and repeat them to yourself, if you allow yourself to be easily derailed from your journey, then use the interruption as evidence to confirm your negativity (I knew in my heart I wouldn't make it), then you can be sure of failure. Your subconscious will cooperate in your opinion of yourself. Fear of failure produces failure if you make it part of your thinking. The conscious mind focuses on the act of failing, and passes the message to the subconscious, which dutifully records and pursues the negative outcome with its million bits per second of power.

An example of worrying about the future might be the case if you were employed by a company and were wrongly anticipating the company's sale and the loss of your position. The more you think about improbable outcomes — "I might lose my job if...." — the more likely the exact outcome you wish to avoid will happen. It is the law of attraction.

Giant Killer Number Three is reliving previous mistakes.

All of us have made stupid mistakes, and every time you relive one of your mistakes, or repeat the entire "stupid" story to someone who probably has little reason to hear it, you strengthen the likelihood of repeating the same mistake. After all, you already know how to make the mistake, so rehashing provides easy direction for the subconscious to follow.

A good friend of Lyle Nelson, against whom he skied in high school, is Mike Deveka, an athlete who was selected for four Olympic teams and won national championships in three different disciplines: cross-country skiing, nordic combined (cross-country skiing and jumping combined), and ski jumping. He also made the United States Cycling Team. To prove that even the best make mental errors (and perhaps to place a final parting shot at a friend who beat Nelson once too often), Nelson relates the following story.

Deveka was in a jumping tournament on the Olympic ski jump at Lake Placid. With the expectation of viewing Deveka soaring picturesquely above the snow, Nelson put on his Olympic jacket, sneaked through crowd control, and found a spot at the top of the landing hill. He glimpsed only a few seconds of Deveka flying through the air, flapping his arms and flailing like a wounded buzzard. He had missed his takeoff and sprung from the lip of the jump much too early. Such a premature launch gives the jumper a sickening feeling of tipping forward, and he must rotate his arms in a forward motion to regain balance. It is not the trademark style of good jumpers.

Deveka's disastrous jump was the first of two, so he had a chance to recover in the standings with a super second launch. As he walked up the hill for his next jump, he saw Nelson and said, "Did you see that blankety-blank first jump of mine? How stupid. You'd think I was some kind of a novice. I must have jumped two meters too soon."

With his expressive negative thoughts in mind, it came as no surprise that Deveka's second jump was a near-perfect replication of the first — another wounded-buzzard flight.

Giant Killer Number Four is the oh-woe-is-me syndrome.

"Well, if you think that was bad, just listen to what happened to me...." People who are in search of attention often seem to be compelled to top the hard-luck story told by a previous let-me-drag-you-down-to-my-level narrator. Misery loves company, but don't let it be your company. Also, be extremely cautious about dragging other people down when you are having a bad day. If you need help, ask for it instead of dispersing negative waves. In reality, your life isn't as bad as you may think at times. Few people would willingly toss their lot into a fishbowl and draw the lot of somebody else in exchange. Remember, you are limited or expanded by how you think.

During Nelson's swift-of-foot years, when he lined up in the front row at a big running race, he could not miss the greetings runners gave to each other. They always amused him:

"Hi, Frank, how have you been?" Frank's response: "Actually, I haven't recovered from the ten-mile run I did on Wednesday and will just have to do today what I can."

The self-put-downs that reached Nelson's ears included: "I'm still feeling down from the cold I had last week." Or, "The baby kept me awake all night, and I'm about to fall asleep on my feet."

Such conscious thoughts tell the subconscious to make the body feel bad, and, of course, it has the power to do so.

"File your excuses ahead of time," is a common joke on the athletic circuit of any sport. Good coaches, however, stop this practice immediately. Anyone who is spending his pre-event time focusing on the excuse, will perform in a manner consistent with making the excuse come true.

Giant Killer Number Five is lounging in the comfort zone.

Humankind has been genetically destined to live with two opposing built-in self-management philosophies. On one hand, we adhere to familiar living patterns and the assurance that tomorrow will be just like today. The body is governed by the rule of homeostasis: return everything to normal; 98.6 degrees today and 98.6 degrees tomorrow. On the other hand, we like to stretch our horizons, to be explorers and to discover a better life. When the homeostatic self gains too much ascendance over the explorer self, we lose our innate courage to take risks and seek new ways to lead our lives. An excessive need for homeostasis also is a major contributor to fear of failure (along with a tarnished self-image and unpleasant memories of failure stored in the subconscious).

Let's review a dramatic statement we made earlier: The only discipline you need is control over what you think about! The information presented above about giant killers shows how we create exactly what we don't want by misplacing our focus. What, then, are the thought processing skills that keep our conscious mind glued to the outcomes we want? Listed below are eight skills which can enhance your personal effectiveness by directing and maximizing the power of your mind. Not one of the eight is difficult to understand or implement. We have chosen to call these skills "self-actualizers." It's ironic that we have to learn to implement these skills, for we are engineered to be successful. The eight skills we have identified are nothing more than the engineered traits we possess and need to recognize. All too often we suppress them by raising unnatural structures and institutions that thwart their potential for extraordinary performance.

Self-Actualizers

Self-Actualizer Number One: Affirmations.

An affirmation is a positive statement that confirms an outcome the individual desires to achieve. Examples of affirmations are:

I will make this year the best year of my life.
I make other people feel good about themselves.
I will establish twenty new accounts each month.
I am an outgoing person who comfortably speaks in public.

If you repeat your affirmations to yourself frequently (ideally six times a day), your reticular operating system (RAS) automatically alerts all components of the mind to watch for opportunities to make the affirmations come true. As one of Lyle Nelson's closest friends, an Olympic teammate, Peter Dascoulias, used to say frequently: "Lyle, you are the luckiest person I have ever met. You are always standing in the right place."

Nelson's luck wasn't accidental; he worked hard (as in the harder you work the luckier you get) to achieve success. He was lucky because his mind was always affirming the outcomes he wanted, and, as a result, he saw opportunities which otherwise would have gone unnoticed.

As we mentioned earlier, the self-image — which mirrors your beliefs and the world — will change if it is constantly being bombarded with new beliefs. Repeated often enough, an affirmation can become a new belief. If you were to speak the affirmation, "I am relaxed and in control when I speak in public," it may not be true the first time you say it. Affirmations speak to your potential to perform, more than your current state of perfection. But even at the beginning, stating an affirmation improves your capability because it focuses desire. If you repeat this affirmation enough times, you will gradually begin to see yourself on the stage comfortably speaking to a large audience.

Affirmations are one of the strongest weapons in your personal change arsenal, but as powerful as they are, you should not rely solely on them to sculpt the self that you want. When used in conjunction with visualization, goal setting, proper planning, values clarification, spiritual orientation through centering, and the expanding energy which humans inherently have, affirmations can be extremely effective.

Self-Actualizer Number Two: Clearly Defined Goals.

Without clearly defined goals, putting yourself through affirmations, visualization and centering is like saying "Giddap" to a horse, then failing to signal which direction you want him to go. Goal setting is indispensable to the achievement of the outcomes you wish for. Clearly defined goals direct the focus of the conscious mind to those activities which, in moments of clearest thinking, you have determined have priority in your life. It is amazing how many opportunities your subconscious, with the help of the RAS, can "see" to make your goal come true.

Everyone who sells a product or service knows that when he or she concentrates on the goal of finding new markets, dozens of unforeseen outlets magically seem to appear. The more targeted your thoughts are about a goal, the better your subconscious can apply the genius within to help you make your objective come true.

Goal setting is crucial for another reason, one that is at the root of most of the mental suffering in America: When the subconscious is not presented with goals and a course of action, it assumes that everything "out there" is important. It converts its power to a ubiquitous scanning of the external environment in search for a sense of priority and order. This constant, non-directed scanning is unsettling to the individual; it may give you a sense of being lost and without meaning.

When you can't channel your energy, the subconscious does not lie idle; it spins its wheels, so to speak, resulting in feelings of frustration and uneasiness. Our survival as a species isn't because of our physical strength, speed, or ability to hide. Our goal-striving character is the major built-in trait which has enabled us to survive and prosper in the earth's deserts and jungles, and you must put your goal-striving skills to work to guide you through today's technological jungles and spiritual deserts.

Another powerful benefit of setting meaningful and challenging goals is their reflection on you. If you respect your goals and view them as inspiring, then you will probably feel the same way about yourself. The act of setting believable goals raises the self-image. You will see yourself in a higher light if your goals are elevated above your current position in life.

Self-Actualizer Number Three: Visualization.

Information is loaded into your subconscious more effectively through images than through words. We convert "word thoughts" to images which effectively conjure up powerful emotional states. By creating positive images and positive emotions (and visualization is the skill of creating images) you can control the composition of your subconscious. The subconscious has to be fed and nourished, and focusing on positive images is the best way to feed the subconscious.

The behavioral sciences were changed forever when plastic surgeon Maxwell Maltz accurately observed that "Your mind cannot distinguish the difference between that which has actually happened and that which is vividly imagined." Imagining unpleasant events or negative outcomes will only distort the self and fixate an unpleasant outlook.

Think of the damage done when a coach walks up to the athlete and asks, "What went wrong?" Answering that question will recreate the images that led to a poor performance, and by reliving them in detail, the subconscious stores them as a representative of the "real you." The next time the poorly performing athlete is in a similar contest, you can bet his subconscious will serve up the same information that caused his original defeat. The opposite of this can be seen in the Workshop of the Mind, which we introduced earlier. Since the mind cannot distinguish between a real happening and an imagined experience, projecting an "improved you" can become an absolute reality when you visualize the idea often enough.

Few, if any, understand the power of the mind better than Lanny Bassham, world-champion shooter and Olympic gold medalist. During one of his Mental Management Seminars, Lanny described a shooting match in which he hit fifty-eight "tens" out of sixty shots to set a world record of 598 out of a possible 600. One of his seminar attendees asked Lanny, "What were you thinking when you shot those two 'nines'?"

Lanny's reply was, "Do you really want to know how I hit two nines, or would you rather hear how I hit fifty-eight tens? I can't remember hitting the nines because I learned from them. Then, knowing that it wasn't like me to shoot a nine, I discarded the memory."

You have to be very conscientious about letting other people load images in your mind which you don't want. If you wish to be a winner, don't hang out with associates who cut you down rhetorically, whether in good humor or not. Comments such as, "Hey, wake up that other peanut in your head and maybe you can understand what's going on," create negative images that whittle down your positive self. Every person visualizes constantly; just make sure you are creating the outcomes you wish to happen.

Self-Actualizer Number Four: Planning.

As you plan, you are creating a goal or event; you are thinking about how to bring about the outcomes you want. Planning requires focus; and focus, as we have discussed, unleashes the potential of the mind. When you have a plan, the Reticular Activating System (RAS) will alert you to all relevant information that could help you accomplish the plan. Without plans and goals, the RAS doesn't know what is significant for the future and what isn't. Planning also changes the filters through which you see the world. Without a plan, you won't really know how, or if, you can accomplish a particular feat. With a logical plan in place — a plan that breaks a project into doable step-by-step tasks — your belief that you are capable of performing the goal increases. Then, when an opportunity to accomplish any part of the plan is presented, the conscious passes the opportunity through the self-image filter, which, because of the believable plan, now reacts positively and sounds a go-for-it message.

Self-Actualizer Number Five: Create an Environment That Fosters Praise and Encouragement.

If you live in a negative environment, associating with people who have a low opinion of themselves, then their attitudes are bound to influence you. Often, the first big step to self-actualization is to turn your back on what is in order to participate in what can be. Remember, it is much easier to change yourself than to change somebody else.

Self-Actualizer Number Six: Focus on the Rewards, Not the Sacrifices.

Many people trap themselves in a "poor me" frame of mind by focusing on what they've had to give up in life. Everybody has to pay a price for success; that's how life is. But if you take the attitude that life's unfair to you by comparing yourself to others who, you think, may have had it easier, you are inviting enmity into your life. Focus instead on what you have accomplished, congratulate yourself on where you are, and make a point of creating new rewards as objectives to work toward.

Self-Actualizer Number Seven: Acknowledge Your Spiritual Nature.

During the last three decades, a great number of studies have been undertaken to determine the distinguishing characteristics of self-actualized men and women: self-actualized being defined as operating at the highest levels of personal potential. A finding common to these studies is that self-actualized individuals — to a greater extent than "average" performers — display three traits that collectively make up a spiritual dimension in the person. These traits are:

1. An obligation to do the morally right thing.
2. A belief that life has a purpose
3. A strong sense of individuality, but a realization that all individuals are a part of a grander order.

Possessing the above traits enables us to regard ourselves in high esteem; it is easy to respect ourselves when our pursuits are invariably just and directed toward our unique "calling".

Self-Actualizer Number Eight: Maintain Your Magic Carpet.

You possess a magical vehicle that can take you to the four corners of the world, to the top of the highest mountains and to the floor of the ocean's coral reefs. The same vehicle, without your slightest involvement, fights tiny dragons attacking you from within (the immune system protecting you from virus and germ invaders). Yes, your body is a miraculous vehicle and deserves to be treated with the care and reverence you would bestow on a magic carpet.

It doesn't matter whether you consider yourself to be a body with a soul, or a soul with a body; either way, your body is vital to your evolution of becoming all that you can be. With this in mind, the reason we believe it is so important to take care of the body is: It is bodily energy that allows you to transport your mental and spiritual strengths to where you want to use them for as long as is earthly possible.

In his play, *The Importance of Being Earnest,* Oscar Wilde wrote a delightful line: "I never travel without my diary. One should always have something sensational to read on the train."

We think this sentiment is a great way to close this chapter with the observation that positive mind control will make you "sensational." The brain only responds to positive or negative thoughts furnished by the mind. So make of yourself a sensational human by believing that you are. Once you remove the idea of smallness you may have placed on yourself, you'll discover the sky is your limit.

As we know, everything is subject to change, and that includes the hardware of the mind. If the conscious mind repeatedly sends a new and empowering message to the self-image, the self-image begins to change and ultimately will accept the newer message as its new filter. Once the filter has been changed, a new set of information reaches the subconscious. The subconscious does not normally change immediately with the new information (although professionals know techniques that in fact can create instant and lifelong change): the stronger the loading of the prior information, the longer it will take for the new information to become dominant in the subconscious. Once it does change, the inner self of the individual is changed, and changing the inner self is how we change our world. Reality to the individual is not an external set of circumstances, but rather reality is our inner interpretation of the external environment.

Replacing our confining filter with filters (beliefs) that more accurately reflect the truth about ourselves and our world is only one way that we grow in awareness. Another growth process that moves us closer to reaching our ultimate self is to actually increase the size (effectiveness and computing power) of each component. Your senses can be trained, for example, to pick up more information. The trained ear can determine what musical pitch the horn of a car makes; the trained olfactory system can distinguish the various brands of perfume. Wine connoisseurs are legendary for their sophisticated palates.

9

Awakening Yourself to the Source of Spiritual Energy

In Western cultures we tend to believe only in those things that can be proved by empirical science. For example, before Columbus the world was flat, before the microscope germs did not exist. Only fifty years ago the limit of the universe was the edges of the Milky Way galaxy. Today's telescopes have expanded awareness to include the hundred billion other galaxies now evident through our lengthened sight.

Empirically we have no way of confirming that energy can be sent from one person to another, or transferred from a universal source to an individual. Or that a primary signal connects all living things. Does this lack mean that spiritual energy or such a phenomenon as one person protecting another with his thoughts (prayers) are myths?

As authors we don't know the answer, but we do know that to restrict our level of acceptance only to that which is proven scientifically is limited thinking. Limited thinkers do not make breakthroughs or expand the horizons of the self or those of humankind. This chapter relates two remarkable stories, not unlike many stories that ask the questions, "What is really possible for the spiritually sensitive and trained?" and, "How are we linked to other living creatures and things?"

As you ponder these questions for yourself, know that it is crucial to human evolvement not to categorically deny that which cannot be seen. Retaining an open mind is to leave open the doorway to human growth.

In this chapter you are going to meet a remarkable woman who is one of the world's leading expedition kayakers. Since she was fourteen years old, kayaking has been her medium for exploring the world, her meditation for discovering herself, the tool of her trade as a river guide.

The course of athletics that Arlene Burns chose, riding the white water of wild rivers, does not lead to the Olympic podium. "I would never belittle the achievement of winning an Olympic gold medal," said Burns, "but the meaning of sports, especially kayaking for me, supercedes the thrill of one-on-one competition. Rather that get psyched up to compete, I must clear my mind of any distractions that impair me from tuning into the river. Often my life, and the those who I am guiding, depends on my physical and mental attunement."

In her roaming of wild rivers on six continents, Burns has probably paddled more miles on the earth's watery arteries in thirty-six years than Carl Lewis has run in preparing to win nine gold medals. Rather than gold, Arlene's excursions have rewarded her richly with friends and many exotic acquaintances; she has exchanged soul thoughts with Tibetan lamas, united Russian and Japanese adversaries by organizing the first Japanese expedition to the disputed Kural Islands, she has collaborated with television producers on adventure films and acted as Meryl Streep's trainer and stunt double in the motion picture, *The River Wild.* We are introducing her to you because her story confirms what can happen to an individual who opens herself to the awakening of her spirit. Her vision of the universal spirit incorporates the river as a metaphor for interacting with the polar elements (positive/negative, male/female, turbulent/calm) inevitably found in life.

"Rivers are the paths of least resistance," Burns says. "They are the arteries that connect thunderclouds to oceans. Whether I am descending waterfalls or drifting through quiet pools, my own energy is synchronized with the energy of the river. Even when immersed in the chaotic turbulence of class five water, it is possible to blend with the force of the river and find a harmony with it."

The "harmony" to which Arlene Burns referred is the one described by Sri Aurobindo, the Indian mystic and philosopher who wrote in his book, *The Life Divine:*

"There must be something in us — much vaster, profounder, truer than the superficial consciousness — which takes delight impartially in all experiences; it is that delight which secretly supports the superficial mental being and enables it to persevere through all labors, sufferings and ordeals … in ordinary life this truth is hidden from us or only dimly glimpsed at times or imperfectly held and conceived. But if we learn to live within, we infallibly awaken to this presence within us which is our more real self, a presence profound, calm, joyous … of which the world is not the master."

Burns' awakening to the power within began in the most implausible manner, when, as a little girl, she was subjected to the mischievous tormenting of her older brother, who, under the guise of babysitting, would frequently lock Burns in the closet for an extended period, thereby liberating himself to join neighborhood friends. The threat of dire punishment if she talked was sufficient to keep Arlene from revealing her ordeal.

Instead of developing a phobic reaction to the dark during the months of repeated confinement, the nine-year-old learned that she could endure the distress by embracing the quietude and finding peace within it — a mental technique that transformed negative emotions into positive response. The same technique, which was a rudimentary form of meditation, helped Burns remain resilient as she departed from a house torn by family strife and walked to a school replete with the pressures that greet all kids who are out of step with their age peers. It was by repeating to herself the mantra-like saying "respond with love, respond with love" that the remarkably self-sufficient child could arrive at school with a sense of confidence and compassion.

By the time she was fourteen, Burns had developed a sense of self-sufficiency far beyond her years. Her ability to take care of herself, to make important decisions and to safeguard her emotional well-being, was demonstrated when she left her mother's house and took up residence in a tree house she built in the woods near her school.

Burns demonstrated her independence by earning extra money selling hand-tooled leather bracelets. She did yard work and other chores to add to her earnings. Whether she realized it or not, Burns' persistent show of independence was a discipline that would prove invaluable to her when she was called upon in later years to exercise quick thinking and sound judgment to escape hazardous situations — in more than one case, to save her life.

By her sixteenth year, Burns' mental exercises had become daily practice, and she reveled in the physical joy of running: her body obeying like an efficient machine, her mind floating freely. It was during these sessions of intense physical motion — later to be replaced by the smooth motion of kayaking — that Burns deeply sensed that there must be something inside her much vaster, profounder, truer than she knew or could explain. Burns began to understand that in knowing this "special something inside us" we become awakened fully to our true nature.

Having directed her own course and having chosen river running and rock climbing as the expression of her spirit, by the time Burns was twenty she had gained know-how and boating wisdom in the boundary waters of Canada and on treacherous flows in the South, including the tricky Chattooga River on which the movie, *Deliverance,* was filmed.

When Burns graduated from the University of South Carolina with a degree in geology, she didn't give a second thought to lucrative offers from rich petroleum companies. With a one-way ticket and $600, she was bound for New Zealand, a mecca for white water enthusiasts. New Zealand would become the first leg in an unplanned, thirteen-year-long journey which would take her to the steppes of Russia, to the heights of Mount Everest and the purple summits of Patagonia, from the hogbacks of China to the back of beyond on calamitous rivers in Nepal. It was both the serene moments in remote villages and perilous escapades in the outbacks that taught Burns how little she knew, how much there was to learn, and how eager she was to assimilate the long-accepted knowledge from diverse cultures.

"In Thailand, where I spent about eight winters, every afternoon I paddled straight out — maybe ten miles — pointing my kayak at the setting sun that became a huge orange orb as it sank into the humid horizon of the tropics. I just drifted and watched the sun disappear, the dying light was renewal for me, a disappearing smile from God, an assurance that She would light up the sky and my heart again the next morning. I paddled home in the dark, guided more by feel than by sight. My boat sliced like a whisper through the silent water.

"This evening ritual was the ultimate form of meditation. I was in a boundless ocean and my world seemed to stretch to the only visible bodies — the stars. It was like a magic spell; although my body was an infinitesimal speck in the whole scheme of things, my mind felt united with the cosmic grace."

After several years of wandering, Burns found her heart and soul's home in the country and people of Nepal where she organized river rafting and trekking expeditions for Americans. She settled into a cycle which found her in Nepal in the fall, Thailand in the winters and lengthy excursions into Russia in the summer, where she guided on rivers and learned to speak the language.

In 1990, after traveling the world for ten years, Burns returned to North Carolina for a three-week lecture tour. There she met a man who helped save her life when it was imperiled four months later. It was from his self-assurance and insightfulness that Burns realized she was ready to take the next step in her spiritual awakening.

The happenstance that brought Burns to seventy-four-year-old Ralph White, a grizzled, retired sea captain who had sailed the Pacific Ocean in the 1920s, was a river guide named Carrie, with whom Burns had worked as a teen. At the time she renewed her acquaintance with Carrie in North Carolina, Burns had been planning a horseback trip that would originate in Siberia and proceed across Mongolia. She was surprised when Carrie said to her, "Arlene, something terrible is going to happen to you on your trip."

The ominous prediction alarmed Burns who, aware that her friend possessed apparent psychic abilities, asked Carrie what she expected to happen. Carrie replied that she had to think about the threat overnight and the next morning informed Burns that there was a man she should meet who would know more about the danger ahead for her.

Burns found Ralph White to be a quiet-spoken spiritual man who had studied yoga for forty years with a sagacious Indian mystic. Impressed with White's calm assurance, and the feeling that he spoke with honesty and directness, Burns was troubled when he said to her, "You will encounter great difficulty during your upcoming journey."

Burns envisioned the dangers always present in the wilds of the Gobi Desert — perhaps she would be unable to find water or her horse would be injured, lost, or stolen.

White did not furnish any details about the perils Burns would encounter, but he told her that he sensed she would survive the experience which was an initiation of sorts. The incident, he added, would enable her to enter another dimension now unknown and unavailable to her.

As she parted from White, he said to her, "Remember, if you need help, call me, I can hear you."

"Sure," Burns chuckled to herself as she imagined the absurd possibility of stumbling upon a telephone booth in the wilderness of Mongolia. "I'll just drop in a quarter and call this old man in the mountains of North Carolina."

Though Burns did not make the trip to Mongolia as planned, she did find herself a few weeks later in the mountainous republic of Tajikistan, formerly the Tadzik Soviet Socialist Republic, which lies in the heart of Central Asia. Bordered by Afghanistan on the south and by the Uygur autonomous region of Sinkiang of China on the east and north, it is a desolate country elevated in the most part above ten thousand feet and drained by a dense river network.

It was in Tajikistan that Burns encountered the perverse attitude held by Muslims toward Westerners. She discovered that men arguing over the price to pay for the one-time usage of "the American woman," her, reflected the lack of respect of Muslims for females.

In Dushambe, the capitol of Tajikistan, she was offered as little as the equivalent of twenty-five cent for her body. More often a goat, sheep or burrow was considered fair payment.

She had been surprised by the level of her resentment for the men. She could remember being truly angry only a few times in her life. Now, she recognized that their hostile attitudes were able to push a button in her that she hadn't known existed. She decided that she must rise above her anger and try to respond in a more appropriate manner, to return their scorn with unconditional love and compassion.

While in Tajikistan, Burns accepted an invitation to join a group of Russians for an exploratory river expedition in neighboring Uzbeckistand and embarked on a forty-hour train ride which originated in Dushambe and cruised along the Afghan border before heading north to the city of Tashkent.

In route she encountered a train full of overly curious Uzbecks: "Are you married?" one asked.

"Of course," she joked, communicating in Russian which is the shared language of the former Soviet Republics. "I have five husbands. One is taking care of the children, one is a gourmet chef, another has a black belt in karate, the fourth cleans the kitchen and the fifth does the laundry." Several of the men stared incredulously, not sure whether to believe her or not.

The persistent questions continued until Burns eventually became weary and concerned about the direction the questions were taking. Particularly repulsive was a fat man who, wanting to impress his fellow travelers, encouraged other males to gather around and delight in his offensive sexual innuendoes. As a means of asserting control and power, he demanded to see Burns' passport. Her refusal affronted his status, and Burns sensed danger in him. The fact that the train was crowded, leaving little opportunity for belligerence, offered her some solace. (It was much later that she realized that no one would have come to her rescue. In their eyes, she was an irreverent, blond-haired, attractive American woman whose morals were obviously flexible or she would not have dared to travel unescorted through the dark of the night.)

Having been assigned a bottom bunk, which also served as the bench seat for other travelers, she had no place to go until everyone else decided to retire. Deciding to extricate herself from the progressively forward men, Burns spotted what seemed to be a safe option and climbed into the luggage rack just below the ceiling. She was too tired to resist sleep, yet too alarmed to allow herself to slip into a deep, unconscious slumber.

Her eyes could not have been closed for ten minutes when she was suddenly awakened by the heavy pressure of someone crawling on top of her. Instincts made Burns' actions quick and reactive. She twisted to the side, drawing her right leg up to her body, and then with all her strength smashed her foot into the dim-lit face of the bearded intruder. As he flipped violently off the luggage rack and crashed to the floor with a loud thump, she realized it was the obnoxious fat man who had earlier been the primary instigator of the sneering sexual remarks.

Infuriated, he jumped to his feet, screaming with indignation and anger, and yanked open the wide window located below the luggage rack above the double row of bunks. He grabbed Burns' legs and pulled down viciously, forcing the lower portion of her body through the open window.

"My God," Burns thought, "he's trying to throw me out of the train! He's trying to kill me!"

Dangling out of the window, she was conscious of the clacking wheels rolling on hard steel five feet below. She realized that she was a moment away from death, that no one in the outside world would have any knowledge of her whereabouts or fate. She hung by her fingers from the inside window sill before finding purchase with her foot. Then, she catapulted herself back through the window and scrambled up to her perch in the luggage rack.

That was the moment when Burns, looking down, took in the sly, expectant, upturned faces of the men who had earlier delighted in the uninvited and unsavory sexual bantering. With sinister eyes and smirking grins, they stared up at her reflecting their anticipation of what was going to happen to her. Many made lewd sexual gestures. They circled like wolves.

Burns estimated that it was close to one in the morning when, cornered like a treed cat on the high luggage shelf, she realized fully that not one single soul among the sixty or so persons on the train was going to come to her aid. In this part of the world, as the men were demonstrating, a Western woman was vulgar, an object of scorn, a sexual adventure to be used and shared with derision, then discarded. For a native woman to come to the defense of an *infidel,* an unworthy female, was unheard of.

When the full impact of her perilous situation struck her, Burns, rather than becoming angry, instead grew clearheaded. She cast rapidly in her mind for resources and decided she would have to fight a delaying action until the men tired of trying to dislodge her or they lost enthusiasm over the novelty of raping a Western woman. The train was due in Tashkent by dawn. If she could repel the men until the light of day, until they tired of the game ... she might save herself. She faced with unflinching honesty the horror that would happen to her if she were dislodged. One false move on her part, one miscalculation as she defended her position on the baggage shelf, and she would fall. She knew she was not exaggerating what would happen if she collapsed into the arms of the frenzied men.

Because she had no weapons with which to attack or defend herself, Burns relied on the center of calm she always called upon when boating through treacherous waters in her kayak. Time after time, she had quieted her thundering heart and frightened imagination by entering her calming center. Now, she placed herself in that strength and visualized around her body an invisible circle of light, a shield of power that could not be punctured by the grasping hands that tried to dislodge her. And that was the moment she remembered the promise of Ralph White to help her and his instructions for her to concentrate on his face. When Burns called up the calm visage of the sea captain twelve thousand miles away, immediately she felt less vulnerable, more certain of a positive outcome to her vigil.

Again and again during that long night Burns repelled the men who leaped and grabbed at her, who tried to capture a hand or foot inevitably extended beyond the shelf. As the night wore on, she fought against the aching fatigue in her body, and when the morning light finally came, she was still crouched on the high shelf. One by one, the men began gathering their belongings in preparation for arrival in Tashkent. Most of them left their seats without a backward glance. One or two looked at her and shrugged as they passed down the aisle.

When finally the locomotive whistled into the station at Tashkent, with blowing steam, screeching brakes and noisy couplings, Burns waited until the car she occupied was completely empty before descending. She had survived, and though she was not to discover until months later, she felt that the power of the circle of light with which she protected herself had a source that was both inside and outside of herself.

Six months after the gang rape attempt on the train, Burns received a letter from her friend, Carrie, who lived in Columbia, South Carolina. It was a response to the one Burns had written describing her ordeal on the train. In it she had reported to Carrie that in her determination to survive she had reached out in her thoughts to every person in her life who might give her strength to resist.

"I knew I needed help," she confessed. "Then I thought about that old guy, Ralph White, you introduced me to. I remembered him saying to me that if I got into trouble to call on him, to visualize his face. It's hard to explain, but

when I concentrated on him I started feeling stronger, and I
fashioned this bubble of white light around myself. It was
like a protective shield, and though I could see no way out
of the heinous situation, I felt better. Then, at last, the
morning came and I was still alive."

Burns saved Carrie's letter because she valued the
message in it highly and because it offered one kind of
personal proof to her of the effects of protective thoughts
projected from one person to another over a long distance:

"On the day you were in trouble on the train,
September 1," Carrie had written, "I had you on my mind.
Then I got a call from Ralph White. He said to me,
'Arlene's in trouble. She's calling us. She needs our help.'

"Both of us dropped everything. I got a babysitter for
the kids, and Ralph and I went to his special place high up
on the mountain behind his house. We stayed there for eight
hours and meditated, sending our thoughts to form a circle
of light around you."

The all-day period in which Ralph White and Carrie
meditated for Burns' safety corresponded exactly with the
eight hours Burns fought off her attackers on the train.

Much later, when Burns returned to North Carolina
and visited with Carrie and Ralph White, he told her that the
image he and Carrie projected to protect her was called "a
cosmic whirlwind;" basically, a moving, spiraling sphere of
intense, all-encompassing energy.

Burns said the force described by Ralph White has
intrigued science for years and is called psychokinesis, the
distant influence of thoughts on a targeted subject.

"The whole experience made me realize," she said,
"that we are each other's fairy dust. It's what the Christians
call prayer, basically the channeling of energy, and
Christians go through God. It doesn't matter what we call it.

It is real. I started realizing what prayer is, in a real sense. I was raised with a Christian background, and now I know that we human beings are completely capable of connecting on an energy level that is not a tangible thing. You can't measure it. People who don't understand this power are often frightened or threatened by the concept. But it's there and it exists and it happens often between parents and children. There are stories about parents who can sense what's happening with their kids from a thousand miles away. Also vice-versa. I think it's fairly common with people who love each other dearly and feel these things that happen from a distance. But it's still something of which people are apprehensive in our society. In India and Asia, telepathy and psychokinesis are integral to the experience of life.

"Americans are always impressed with statistics," Burns said. "Give us some facts backed by scientific research, and we believe. Awakening came to me in a cumulative fashion. If I were to attempt to pinpoint a day, or time, or one event, which may have been responsible for awakening my sense of spiritual transformation, it was probably that night on the train in Central Asia. But it was like a major piece fitting into an unraveling puzzle.

"I think the human organism is capable of wonders of self-transformation. Sometimes we are tricked into assuming this power. Sometimes, it's guided to us like the force that came to me from Ralph White and Carrie. Or it may be as simple and as complex as the hypnotic elimination of allergies and warts. The self-transformative power available to humans can be specific enough to alter the blood-cell count, powerful enough to remove cancer, or elaborate enough to cause wounds in the hands and feet that only bleed on Good Friday. I know the power can touch people in mysterious ways. But we have to be open to belief. That's when life really begins, when we open our hearts to the music of the spheres."

There are two ways to view Arlene Burns' transformative ordeal on her train ride across Central Asia. The typical Western view is to admire the scrappiness of the woman who was able, against all odds, to defend herself against predatory men for eight hours and relegate the circle of light projected around her to the realm of her imagination.

And this viewpoint is the easiest because it does not challenge us to accept the idea that we just might be more spectacular, less predictable and common, than we are. It is comfortable, certainly not unsettling or challenging, to accept life as it comes to us, becoming neither more nor less than we have to be in order to prosper and get by and to be content with our ordinary beliefs and prejudices. This familiar way of perceiving ourselves does not take the soul into account.

It says to us that we are limited creatures whose minds are confined to our brains and bodies and to the present moment. When all our moments run out, our bodies will die and we will disappear into the abyss of nothingness. What a bleak and terrible destiny!

The alternative to the typical viewpoint of Arlene Burns' salvation and other spiritual events that confound the pragmatic mind is the one described by Larry Dossey in his book, *Recovering the Soul:* "… if minds cannot be bounded in space and time, we must be prepared to admit — whether we feel squeamish about it or not — that we are endowed with the Godlike characteristics of immortality, omnipresence and unity."

Dossey adds further: "But, on the whole, we are not yet fully capable of acknowledging the God-qualities we contain — our 'omniconsciousness,' as Jung called it. To compound this blindness, too often our religious traditions have driven home the message that we are despicable, unworthy creatures with no redeemable qualities of our own. And when, throughout history, individuals have risen who have clearly sensed their inner divinity, they have frequently been accused of heresy and blasphemy and have been treated inhumanely or killed, particularly in the West. These woeful facts reveal the unbelievable lengths to which we will go to hide from our own true nature, and they show that we have habitually confused participation in the godhead with usurpation of the divine.

"Thus was Jung led to the conclusion, late in life, that 'the Christian nations have come to a sorry pass; their Christianity slumbers and has neglected to develop its myth further in the course of the centuries … people do not realize that a myth is dead if it no longer lives and grows … our myth has become mute, and gives no answers. The fault lies not in it as it is set down in the scriptures, but solely in us, who have not developed it further, who, rather, have suppressed any such attempts.'

"Today the question is how to reawaken the old myths, or how to devise new ones. It seems at least theoretically possible to stir the old myths to life — to take seriously the Old Testament idea of 'divine marriage' and the subsequent notion of 'Christ within us'; to take Jesus at his word when he said in John 10:34, 'It is not written in your law, I said, you are gods.' Yet there is such an inertia and resistance to revitalization."

It is individuals like Arlene Burns, and the others we have described in this book — who have experienced self-transformation — that become the witnesses, the pathfinders, for those who require the inspiration to make

changes in themselves. And all of us do require inspiration
to become irrevocably convinced of our divinity, of our self-
transformative potential to be so much more than we are.

Inspiration in a mysterious fashion was the subject of
a fascinating magazine article author Thorn Bacon wrote in
1968 after he met "The Man Who Reads Nature's Secret
Signals." Acknowledged by the editors of *National Wildlife*
magazine to be one of the most popular features ever
printed by the periodical, the story of Cleve Backster later
became the focal point for a national craze in which people
began talking to their plants. "Plants," Bacon wrote, "may
be receptors and messengers of esoteric signals in a
language and form we know nothing about."

The statement referred to Backster's experiments in
his New York offices where, in 1968, he taught polygraph
techniques to members of the New York Police Department.
Formerly an interrogation specialist with the CIA,
Backster's lie detector instruction to cops took a back seat
on a February morning in 1966 when, on a whim, he
decided to measure the rate at which water rose in a dracena
plant in his office from the root area into the leaf. Backster's
own words describe what happened when he attached a pair
of PGR electrodes to each side of a leaf of the plant:

"Contrary to my expectation, from the outset the plant
leaf tracing exhibited a downward trend. Then, after about
one minute of chart time, the tracing exhibited a contour
similar to a PGR reaction pattern typically demonstrated by
a human subject experiencing an emotional stimulation of
short duration. Even though its tracing had failed to reflect
the effect of the watering, the plant leaf did offer itself as a
possibly unique source of data.

"As I watched the PGR tracing continue, I wondered if
there could be a similarity between the tracing from the plant

and a PGR tracing from a human. I decided to try to apply some equivalent to the threat-to-well-being principle, a well-established method of triggering emotionality in humans. I first tried to arouse the plant by immersing a plant leaf in a cup of hot coffee. But there was no measurable reaction.

"After a nine-minute interim, I decided to obtain a match and burn the plant leaf being tested. At the instant of this decision, at thirteen minutes fifty-five seconds of chart time, there was a dramatic change in the PGR tracing pattern in the form of an abrupt and prolonged upward sweep of the recording pen. I had not moved, or touched the plant, so the timing of the PGR pen activity suggested to me that the tracing might have been triggered by the mere thought of the harm I intended to inflict upon the plant. This occurrence, if repeatable, would tend to indicate the possible existence of some undefined perception in the plant."

Backster's experience with the dracena plant that morning in New York led him to an exploration of how the suffering of other species affected his plants. He bought brine shrimp, ordinarily used as live food for tropical fish, and killed them by dumping them into boiling water in a lead-lined room where no electromagnetic signal known to science could penetrate. Yet in another room 150 feet away, where a dracena plant was attached to electrodes, he saw the polygraph recording needle leap frantically. He was awed by a startling and apparently new concept: "Could it be that when cell life dies, it broadcasts a signal to other living cells?" If this was so, he would have to completely automate his experiments, removing all human elements which might consciously or unconsciously contaminate the results.

In the three years following his brine shrimp experiment, Backster spent thousands of dollars transforming his offices into a space-age assembly of mechanized shrimp-dump dishes, a sophisticated electronic randomizer and programmer circuitry, and multiple PGR monitoring devices. But the results continued to point to a capability for perception in all living cells — a perception that Backster called "primary."

Bacon asked him several questions, which were printed in the *National Wildlife* article:

Q: What do you mean by primary?

A: I mean primary in the sense that this perception applies to all cells that we have monitored, without regard to their assigned biological function.

Q: What types of cells have you tested?

A: We have found this same phenomenon in the amoeba, the paramecium, and other single-cell organisms; in fact, in every kind of cell we have tested: fresh fruits and vegetables, mold cultures, yeasts, scrapings from the roof of the mouth of a human, blood samples, even spermatozoa.

Q: Do you mean that all of these cells have a sensing capacity?

A: It seems so. Incidentally, we have tried unsuccessfully to block whatever signal is being received by using a Faraday screen, screen cage, and even lead-lined containers. Still the communication continues. It seems that the signal may not even fall within our electrodynamic spectrum. If not, this would certainly have profound implications.

Q: What kind of signal is it?

A: I can answer your question better by telling you what we think the signal is not. We know it is not within the different known frequencies: AM, FM, or any form of signal which we can shield by ordinary means. Distance seems to impose no limitation. For example, we are conducting research that would tend to indicate that this signal can traverse hundreds of miles.

Q: In the final analysis, aren't you saying that we must reassert our definitions of sensory perception and intelligence?

A: Who can say at this point? There are certainly implications here that could have profound effects on those concepts. Our observations show that the signal leaps across distances, as I said before. I have been as far away as New Jersey — about fifteen miles from Manhattan — and have merely thought about returning to my office, only to learn when I returned that at the precise moment I had had the thought — checked against a stopwatch — there was a coincidental reaction by the plants to the thought of my coming back. Relief? Welcome? We aren't sure, but evidence indicates something like relief. It isn't fear.

The trend of Backster's research results did indeed embrace profound implications. Do plants have emotions? Do they make strange signals of awareness beyond our own abilities to comprehend? It seems so. "Personally," Bacon said, "I can't imagine a world so dull, so satiated, that it should reject out of hand arresting new ideas which may be as old as the first amino acid in the chain of life on our earth. Inexplicable has never meant miraculous. Nor does it necessarily mean spiritual. In this case, it may simply prove to mean another extension of our natural laws."

If Arlene Burns has anything in common with Cleve Backster, it lies within the realm of wonder and awe. Both stories demonstrate the unknown depths of perception and communication in our world. They lead us to strengthen our sense of admiration for who we may turn out to be — far greater than we imagine, with a potential for excellence and elegance we do not, now, even have the ability to measure.

Norman Shealy and Carolyn Myss, authors of *The Creation of Health*, write in their book about the self-transformative potential to become "an elegant spirit." What a lovely concept! We think their definition of an elegant spirit should be shared with everybody who secretly yearns to follow the path of those who have discovered how to transform themselves:

"The principle of healing — of that which creates and maintains health and life — is spirituality in motion. That we create our own realities is the activity of spirituality in motion.

"Even if a person cannot accept the existence of a God or of some form of divine intelligence, nevertheless, the evidence illustrating the connection between human emotions and the condition of the physical body stands as tangible proof that the energy of our consciousness is real. And more than real, it is a creative force.

"What does this information have to offer us in terms of how we live our lives? At the very least, it suggests that to live unconsciously, that is, unaware of what we are thinking, feeling and thus creating, is threatening to our health, not to mention the other areas of our lives. It is simply not productive to deny one's own power. It is, in fact, self-defeating.

"The other option, the higher one, is to learn to live consciously, developing skills of awareness and insight that release a person from having to feel victimized or controlled by life's challenges ever again. This quality of personal power transforms ordinary human consciousness into a force that radiates elegance and grace.

"The presence of a person who is truly 'elegant' is unmistakable. These individuals project an energy which communicates that 'visitors passing through their energy fields' are welcome and safe. The usual barriers created through human insecurities are absent.

"This quality of consciousness is fertile ground for the seeds of unconditional love, an attitude of nonjudgmentalism, and acceptance of all that has life. That is what it means to be an elegant spirit — an individual who has awakened to the realization that he or she is a creator, and therefore acts to honor that power through living with love, wisdom and compassion. This person is an example of what Abraham Maslow calls 'self-actualized.' These are the peacemakers, and they will indeed 'inherit the earth.'"

Inspired by Shealy and Myss' definition of "an elegant spirit," we requested permission to reprint here the suggestions of these authors to all of those who seek to follow the path to becoming an elegant spirit. As a preface to these valuable suggestions, we urge you not to take lightly the idea of living the way of the elegant spirit. Think about the strong dedication of the men and women we have presented in this book — their personal efforts, their sacrifices, their pledges to excellence, their stubbornness to become who they are; their awareness from the start that, far from easy, the path they chose was the one most marked with obstacles. As Shealy and Myss put it, "Becoming an aware human being is a full-time job. At times, you might regret your ever having stepped foot on this path because awareness does not necessarily make your life easier. In fact, it will most certainly bring you challenges that seem to be monumental. To see clearly, to have the inner vision clear enough to penetrate the illusions other people still maintain, can be very discouraging.

"Likewise, to choose a path of awareness is not an intellectual exercise. It is a living, breathing, constant discipline. If you choose to believe that you create your own reality, that perception does not include any vacation time. You must always live in that perception, no matter what the situation, no matter what the challenge. Indeed, your intellect will not be your opponent on this path — your challenges will come from your emotions. It is your emotional warehouse that holds your fears, insecurities and lesser qualities. Healing these inner limitations will be your challenge, again and again."

Here are the fifteen suggestions written by Norman Shealy and Carolyn Myss for those who would take up the challenge to become elegant spirits:

1.   Personal values must be based upon the truth of your origin. You are spirit. You command energy to take form according to your thoughts, feelings and words, and you are responsible for the quality of that which you contribute to the creation of life. It is, therefore, in your own best interest as well as that of others to create with love and wisdom. Keep your words, thoughts and emotions clear and honest.

2.   Universal Principles serve as guidelines for creation: cause and effect, what is in one is in the whole, manifestation is the result of intention. These, and all other Universal Principles, are your power tools. The more you know and understand Universal Principles, the more empowered you become.

3.   Each person who enters into your life is a reflection of some aspect of your own being. Likewise, you are a reflection for each person

also. Whether you are drawn to their positive qualities, or repelled by their negative traits, you are only seeing yourself. This reflection is often difficult to see clearly because the depth of the reflection is usually disguised by the personality of the individual. If you can look beyond the personality traits, you will see yourself in the depths of a person's motivations, fears, strengths and compassion. Blaming others, therefore, serves no purpose.

4. All artificial barriers that separate the essential oneness of life should be disregarded. Boundaries between nations which maintain that certain people are different than others are obsolete, meaningless and serve only to separate people from one another. Allegiance belongs to life itself. Life has no boundaries. It thrives anywhere there is love.

5. Likewise, the boundaries that are now present among all of the other kingdoms of life — animal, mineral and plant — are also artificial barriers that prevent respect, interspecies communication and emotional bonding. All life has consciousness.

6. What is in one is in the whole. Apply this teaching to your life and all that you create, realizing that every positive and negative action you put into motion affects the whole of life.

7. Time and space are nonexistent in the dimension

of thought. Thoughts travel in an instant. Therefore, learn to think in terms of your thoughts as a multi-level communications system in which such activity as healing at a distance can be accomplished.

8.   Because thoughts are power, develop a quality-control checkup on yourself on a regular basis. When you feel that too much negativity is present in your system, do something to heal yourself immediately. Pay attention to the law of cause and effect, and study the consequences of your actions, words and thoughts, realizing at all times that you are the creator behind that which you are studying.

9.   Heal your own addiction to violence in any and every form: actions, attitudes, words, habits and thoughts. Our violent natures create our violent politics, weapons, and all violent human actions and interactions. We all have violence in us. Our world is a violent world, and these proclivities have entered into us through the very air we breathe. Remember that violence breeds disease and destroys the human emotional system.

10.   Study those desires in your life that control you, and strive to release yourself from anything artificial that exerts power over you: drugs, alcohol, negative habits, fears — anything that causes you to lose power.

11.   Remember at all times that you are constantly

healing. The process of healing is a verb and not a noun. Your body is reacting every second to your thoughts, feelings, emotions and experiences. Health is not a permanent condition unless you create it so each day.

12. When you must take time to heal, do it gently. Healing through force of will alone, through determination without self-compassion, is a form of self-inflicted violence. Don't resent your body for breaking down; learn from the experience so that it does not have to be repeated. Trust the process of healing. It has an intelligence of its own. Learn to listen to what your body needs and to what your spirit needs. Above all, value your health and your well-being as your first priority. Honor thyself.

13. Clearly define in your heart your spiritual principles. Know and be clear about what you believe. Do not accept beliefs without question. Keep your focus on yourself and not on others.

14. Set time aside each day for your spiritual practice. Meditation and prayer are essential. Learn to be still and hear the inner voice of your soul.

15. Above all, practice loving. Unconditional love requires the ultimate of efforts and it reaps the ultimate of rewards.

Finally, you must understand that once you start on the path to self-transformation there is no turning back. You cannot make a bargain with the eternal spirit to practice only a half-hearted reunion. Be warned that when you embark on the road to awakening, though you may take detours, you will never be able to return to the person you were before you commenced the great journey.

It was Edna St. Vincent Millay who so grandly caught the meaning of the great journey in resounding words that crash like cymbals in the mind:

> The world stands out on either side
> No wider than the heart is wide;
> Above the world is stretched the sky —
> No higher than the soul is high.
> The heart can push the sea and land
> Farther away on either hand;
> The soul can split the sky in two,
> And let the face of God shine through.

10

Inward Bound with Alexander Everett

Centering and meditation, techniques you will learn about in this chapter, provide us humans with the link we need to unify ourselves with the Good Will *of the universe. By centering, the individual seeks to create in himself a calm balance which not only benefits the human body in many ways, but places the seeker on the path to liberating the spirit. Every aspect of human performance seems to be enhanced when, in centering, the individual spirit joins with the overflowing* Good Will *energy of the universe.*

It takes practice and dedication to make centering a habit. But those we've interviewed who have sought the path of meditation tell us that they have grown stronger mentally and spiritually and more solidly positioned in life as a result of centering. Their horizons have expanded and their sense of who they are and who they can be in relation to the whole of the universe has enlarged to encompass a future without limitations.

In this chapter we are going to introduce you to Alexander Everett, an Englishman who became a United States citizen and later founded Mind Dynamics. This was the organization responsible for turning out the people who started such famous mind-training programs as EST, The Forum, LifeSpring, Life Stream, Context Training, PSI World, Personal Dynamics of Switzerland, Life Dynamics of Japan, and many others.

It is safe to say that Alexander Everett, with his ideas, his personality, the depth of his vision, was the innovator around whom the entire human movement of mental imagery in the United States was staged. He was the center, the inspiration, the thinker who had come from the British Isles. There he was a successful teacher who established Pendragon, a preparatory school in Sussex, England, after which he became headmaster of Shiplake College. But money and high position were not enough for Alexander; he was stirred by a desire to help people clarify themselves, find themselves, discover who they were and how they fit into the world — into the universe.

Though Mind Dynamics was a financial success ("I taught people how to think right, feel right, and act right," said Alexander), it was not enough for the teacher. There were too many people who came to his workshops who failed to learn; they resisted change, returning to ingrained patterns of negativity soon after the "workshop glow" had worn off.

There had to be a better way, Alexander realized, and he found it in the spiritual state of human consciousness. "This represents the God essence within each individual," Alexander said. "It is the universal power, God, within each of us, whatever we choose to call it. And that part is perfect."

It was in 1984 when one of the authors, Thorn Bacon, attended a workshop given by Alexander Everett. There in Alexander's modest house near Eugene, Oregon, among the fir trees, exotic animals and placid lakes that dotted his farm, Bacon heard the transplanted Englishman say, "I am here to show people how to enter a higher state. It is all a matter of becoming more aware of the genius within, developing and using it. We tend to look to powers outside ourselves. I want people to look within. Hence, the title of my seminar — Inward Bound."

Athletes, in common with mystics, probably experience Alexander's inner world — touch upon the magnificence of who we are — more profoundly than many people because the stress on the mind and body necessary to condition the physique for rigorous competition often transports sports figures into the inner world. They may experience often that which Alexander teaches as centering — the technique to go inward bound and merge with the universal spirit.

Authors Murphy and White wrote about athletes experiencing the richness of the inner world when they observed, "As we have seen, a wide variety of extraordinary experience emerges in sport — moments of preternatural calm and stillness, feelings of detachment and freedom, states filled with invincible force. These experiences induce a wide range of extraordinary perceptions, including changes in one's sense of time and space, apparent clairvoyance and telepathy, and glimpses of disembodied entities. This richness of experience is paralleled in the mystical traditions by the knowledge that ordinary human nature opens into vast inner worlds. Various metaphors have illustrated this fact of spiritual life. In the Greek myth of the Minotaur, the path to transformation led through the labyrinth; the seeker, like Theseus, had to find his way with the help of Ariadne's golden thread, which symbolized a teacher's leading. The soul has been pictured as a mansion [Saint Teresa's "Interior Castle"] or as a Magic Theatre [in Herman Hesse's *Steppenwolf*], in which one space opens into many others. Hindu and Buddhist writings describe a multitude of inner worlds. As Sri Aurobindo wrote, 'we have not learned to distinguish the different parts of our being; for these are usually lumped together simply as 'mind'.... Therefore [we] do not understand our own states and actions.... It is part of the foundation of yoga to become conscious of the great complexity of our nature.'"

Murphy and White went on to describe how a veteran of the National Football League, former St. Louis Cardinal linebacker David Meggyesey, fell into a labyrinth of the interior life during his playing days. His adventure began during a practice game against the Minnesota Vikings when he received a blow to the head. In a semi-dazed state, he sat on the sidelines and watched the setting sun beyond the stadium. He felt "an eerie calm and beauty," and had an impression of "outlines wavering gently in the fading light." In this pervasive sense of the uncanny and sublime, he began to see "auras around some of the players." The experience helped trigger other unusual experiences that season. On another occasion he found himself playing in "a kind of trance where I could sense the movements of the running backs a split second before they happened." With this heightened sense of anticipation, he played a brilliant game. But this state led him beyond football.

His extraordinary experiences during that football season opened into a more complete understanding and practice. One inner space led to another. The spontaneous richness of these events led him into yoga and other disciplines, and he eventually evolved his own path to the inner life.

It is the "inner life" that Alexander Everett seeks to explore when he leads spiritual aspirants through the process of getting in touch with the everlasting reality inside themselves, and it is the discovery of how to become inward bound that is the purpose of this chapter. Those who have become inward bound, inner-directed, able to see with less cloudy vision into their own future, find purpose in their lives and a sense of the grand continuity beyond the body. They may experience the exuberant, expansive, smiling-all-over feeling listeners feel when they hear Barbra Streisand sing, "On a clear day, rise and look around you, and see who you are...."

The answer to who we are is a fascinating definition most of us seek. Like David Meggyesey, those of us who find the path to the inner life become expanded humans whose vision is far reaching. As a final step in the journey inward bound, we have turned to Alexander Everett with questions of how to get in touch with the genius inside each of us.

His answers make up the bulk of this chapter and are divided into three sections:

Our Purpose
Centering the Self
The Seven Laws of Life

Dozens of times in this book we have written about athletes who have experienced the zone or the flow. Invariably, these experiences have been described as uplifting or transcending — the individual enters a sphere of calm and a transforming sense of peace and certainty surrounds him. But, as we have also noted, often — in contrast to David Meggyesey — the athlete, or any person, who encounters the spirit without preparation may choose to view the encounter as abnormal, as a freak happening, or, at the very least, as a discomforting experience. To a lesser degree than a few years ago, there is an avoidance of exploration of the spirit in athletes. Many back off, refuse to acknowledge inner sight, or take the attitude that a visit to the zone is a sign of weakness. Yet, the abilities we have described in this book show us that all of us — if we choose — can voluntarily extend our boundaries beyond the physical zone, although one need not be an athlete to touch a higher state of consciousness.

The body, as Alexander Everett explains, is a centering point, a place to start from which to reach beyond, to flesh out the spirit with the grace of understanding our purpose. Once we understand our purpose, why we are here on planet earth, then our individual lives make more sense. We no longer have to stumble through life as if we were wearing blinders. We can become successful people with marvelous futures that extend beyond our limited vision.

We asked Alexander Everett to define in his own words what the human purpose is. Here is what he said:

"Many people never stop to think about the question of purpose, of why do anything in life that's worthwhile. But there is only one answer to the question, 'What is the purpose of life?' Around 500 B.C., Socrates put it in two words, which he had carved above the entrance to his academy: 'Know Thyself.' The whole purpose of life is to know who we are. If we did, we would never be sick, never be poor, never have a bad relationship; we would have the right job, be happy and prosperous. When we get in touch with the power within, we know we are part of God. The whole of God is indivisible and is within you.

"I like to think of this idea as God being an ocean," Alexander said. "You go out in a boat, and for thousands of miles there is ocean. But you can lean over the side and scoop up some of the water with a glass or cup. Now you have sea water that has everything in it that the whole ocean has. Even in one drop of ocean water, everything is in it.

"You're like a glass full of God's ocean. Within that glass you represent everything that's there. You are complete and whole.

"And yet we do not believe it. In response to an awakening soul power in us we attend seminars looking for a list of ingredients in our glass of water. We attend lectures, go to churches, read books and talk to people. And according to how deeply we seek, so do we find. But the key to understanding is that we must allow what we find to become a part of our consciousness. There are millions of seekers; there are a few thousand finders. Only about ten percent of the finders actually realize what they have and how effective they can be."

According to Everett, the spirituality of which he speaks can be known by any person directly through deliberate practices such as prayer or centering the self because we are secretly joined with it already. What we must do is to remove the veil from our eyes. Centering is but one of the techniques.

Before we explain Everett's centering technique and the benefits it brings to everyday life, we think it is worthwhile to look at another view of the spiritual reality to which we are all bound. This is a view probed by the great Carl Jung, whose concept of immortality matches with that of Alexander.

Jung was never more certain than when he asserted that paying attention to the manifestations of the timeless Mind was the redeeming life task for all persons. This task is especially difficult in our era because we have shifted all emphasis to the here and now — to doing, to consuming, to practicality, to material progress. But, as Jung clearly believed, the One Mind cannot be put in a box in the here-and-now because it is infinite and eternal. And because its concept of space and time is different from that which we commonly value we find ourselves cut off from it. The result has been predictable: We have become victims of our own unconscious drives, and a materialization of our world has come about. But our task in life is just the reverse, Jung insisted, "the exact opposite: to become conscious of the contents that press upward from the unconscious" — to "create," as he put it, "more and more consciousness." Only in this way can we realize "the sole purpose of human existence: ... to kindle a light in the darkness of mere being."

Jung, and other enlightened philosophers who followed in the footsteps of his beliefs, did not agree with the tendency of the Western religions to regard the soul as something small, ignominious, unworthy, personal, and subjective. He pointed out the contradictions of this view by questioning how could something so small and unworthy be immortal? — as these religions insist. All around us, he said, there are clues to the contrary — that the soul is magnificently unbounded — and he spent a lifetime accumulating evidence for this. His conclusion: "The soul is assuredly not small, but the radiant Godhead itself."

The connection between the soul and consciousness? Jung came to the conclusion that human consciousness is "the invisible, intangible manifestation of the soul." Thus the task of "creating more and more consciousness" (meaning an expansion of the awareness of the infinity of the God-self) becomes the equivalent of recovering the soul and regaining contact with the inner divinity. But how can this be done?

How can we regain contact with the inner divinity? One answer comes from centering. The centering technique perfected by Alexander Everett brings about several direct benefits as a result of aligning the body with the spirit.

When we center, Alexander explained, we create better health by freeing our intuition to tell us how we need to improve our immune systems. This means exercising properly, eating correctly and doing what we should to keep our bodies strong. We are constantly exposed to germs and diseases. When the immune system is in balance, we are able to ward off illness. If we are centered and feel good about ourselves, we cannot think ourselves ill, Alexander says; we are not going to psychosomatically make ourselves unhealthy. Centering allows us to align with our inner power to stay physically fit.

When we learn to center ourselves and go within, we relax. When we relax there is less stress and it is very easy to get more restful sleep anywhere and at any time.

Another benefit of centering is the release of more happiness. "Happiness is not something we receive later in life when we retire," Alexander says. "It is a means of traveling; a way of life. When we center, we see what we need to do in life. And happiness is fulfilling our purpose."

Longer life is another benefit of centering, Alexander Everett observed. "Man is actually designed to live one hundred twenty years, not the seventy we are accustomed to thinking about. We are programmed to work until we are sixty or sixty-five, then we retire, and five years later we die. But if we program ourselves differently, we can choose our own life spans."

Among the nice things that happen to people who are centered is the appearance of more friends in their lives. According to Alexander, "When we center ourselves and get in touch with who we are, have better health and are more relaxed and happy; others will want to be around us. People relate to what we are — our demeanor, our beingness, our charisma — not to what we say. If we are centered, people will be attracted to us like moths to a candle. Those around us will want to be with us and share with us because we are at one with our inner power."

Another direct benefit of centering is that the individual becomes less accident prone. If we are centered, Alexander pointed out, we are more aware of what is going on around us. Minor awkwardness such as knocking over a glass of water, or a major automobile accident can be avoided when we are aware of our surroundings. If we are aware, we will move the glass of water or get out of the way of the person driving foolishly.

"You see, there really are no accidents in life," Everett said. "They are self-created. You can learn not to create them by being centered and aware."

For persons to whom wealth is important, centering bestows the benefit of more money. Everett said: "When we know our purpose in life, when our work fulfills our unique talent so that we have pleasure in accomplishing our daily tasks, we will be productive, successful and we will make more money. We are paid in direct proportion to what we give, and when we are centered and feel good about what we are doing, we give openly and generously to the world."

Alexander added this thought: "If you say, 'I want to be a millionaire!' do you know what you have to do? Just give one million dollars worth of service and share yourself in a way whereby you are giving one million dollars. Then you will get what you want."

"Don't try to find a quick way to make money, because you will lose it. Oh, you might make it, I'm not saying you won't. But it will not stay with you. The way to make money and to keep it flowing is to have the consciousness of the fact that you are here to serve."

Evidence of the power of centering and meditation to produce marked changes in the body is becoming more widespread. For example, in 1975, the physician Herbert Benson proposed in his best-selling book, *The Relaxation Response,* that by practicing a simple form of meditation (similar but not quite the same as centering), a person can change his heart rate, respiration and brain waves. They slow down with meditation, muscles relax, and the effects of epinephrine and other stress-related hormones diminish. Studies have shown that by routinely seeking "the relaxation response" (by centering or meditating), 75 percent of insomniacs begin to sleep normally. Many women who have been infertile become pregnant, and chronic pain sufferers in about 34 percent of the cases reduce their use of painkilling drugs.

In his latest book, *Timeless Healing,* Benson points out that prayer operates along the same chemical pathways as the relaxation response, providing the power to affect corticosteroid messengers in the body, or "stress hormones," leading to lower blood pressure, more relaxed heart rate and respiration, and other benefits. So does centering, for it embraces the same meditative process of letting go.

According to one authority, David Felton, chairman of the Department of Neurobiology at the University of

Rochester, quoted in a *Time* magazine article on faith and healing, "Anything involved with meditation and controlling the state of mind that alters hormone activity has the potential to have an impact on the immune system."

There is no question but that centering on a regular basis not only brings the physiological benefits of the "relaxation response," but it provides the qualitative mindset for solving life's vexing problems with greater personal equanimity.

Alexander Everett advises that centering should become a habit.

"We all need to center every day for at least fifteen minutes. If we do just fifteen minutes per day, the balance of the twenty-four hours will be much more in harmony. The best time to center is early in the morning. Perhaps you like to do your chores first — tend to the cat and dog, brush your teeth and so forth — or perhaps you like to center when you first get out of bed. Create your own magic."

Based on information concerning the physical posture most conducive to centering, Alexander said that it seems more natural for us as Westerners to sit in a chair with our feet flat on the floor. If you want to take your shoes off, do so. Arms and legs should be uncrossed. You can sit on the floor, but make sure your spine is straight — and your back is against the wall. The energy flows through the base of the spine upwards, and if the spine has a kink in it, the energy is obstructed.

The peace and quiet that you can find in the centering process comes about as a result of stilling your body. To enter the fourth state of consciousness, you have to still the body, still the emotions, still the mind, to enter the place where peace is.

The following explanation of Alexander Everett's centering technique is based on utilizing the seven colors of the rainbow.

According to Alexander, when a white light passes through a prism, the seven colors of the rainbow are formed. These represent the seven aspects of God. The Old Testament calls it the Elohim God, which are the seven rays of Elohe or God. God comes at seven levels, and He awakens our bodies at seven points. In India, these points are called chakras. The chakras and the colors of the rainbow help activate the highest part of us.

The lowest part is the color red, located on the outermost band of the rainbow. The highest is violet, the innermost color. So we go from red to violet to reach our innermost part of being. Red represents the physical part, the external. The next color, orange, is the emotional part, the color expressing feeling. Yellow symbolizes the mental. The fourth color is green, the color of peace. In order to reach the green peaceful state, you have to quiet the red physical part of you, calm the orange emotional part, and still the yellow mental part so that you can enter the fourth spiritual state.

The fifth color is blue, which represents love. Purple is the mental level of spirituality — the knowing level of the masters. Violet represents the spiritual-spiritual, where consciousness becomes one with God.

All of the colors, Alexander explained, are psychological trigger devices, a method to bring the individual peace by centering himself. Centering is not the only method of coming to peace, of course. It is the one Alexander uses, "because I wanted to find something that did not clash with Buddhism, Hinduism, Christianity, Judaism or any religion. Every religion will accept the colors of the rainbow. Every religion will accept nature. I have tried to create a universal spiritual language."

The Centering Procedure

Now you can begin the actual steps of centering yourself. You start with the color red and progress, as you move deeper into yourself, to the color violet.

Following is an explanation Alexander Everett has written to take you step by step inward bound:

First, close your eyes and visualize the seven colors of the rainbow. You might wish to create a rainbow in your mind's eye and imagine yourself passing from the outside band of red inward toward violet. Slowly, as if you were a traveler on a quiet journey of self-discovery, pass through red, orange, yellow, green. Depending on your visualization powers, you may actually see the different colors vividly as you progress through the rainbow stages. Your passage should be slow and silent, free of mind clatter and interruptions. Start your centering exercise by saying to yourself:

I now prepare to center myself. The first color I will visualize is red. I will actually see the color red in my mind, and in sequence as I progress, I will visualize the other colors of the rainbow.

Red:
I first will visualize the color red. I relax my body from head to foot. I relax, let go of my body. Relax.

When you release the muscles around the eyes, the throat area and the lungs, the rest of the body will let go.

Orange:

> *I next visualize the color orange. I release and let go of all of my emotions. I desire only that which is good for others.*

To forget yourself and your desires, direct your energy into the desire to help others. Put aside your own desires and say,

> *I want to help my fellow man the best way I can.*

When you do this your personal desires and needs become less.

Yellow:

> *I calm and still my mind, I bring my mind to rest.*

This is the statement you say to yourself. To still the mind, see yourself somewhere in nature — in a park, by a river, in the desert, in a garden — wherever it is natural for you to be. When the mind is surrounded by nature, your thinking slows down, you become more peaceful.

Green:

> *I allow peace to come into my life. I sense a state of peacefulness within every cell of my body.*

Now you can enter peace: you have stilled your body, stilled the emotions and stilled the mind.

Blue:

> *I let love permeate my entire being. I feel myself full of love.*

Many people cannot love because they are not at peace. How can you love when you are upset mentally, physically and emotionally? Peace comes before love.

Purple:

> *I seek out the depths within. I aspire to that inner secret place.*

Purple is the master level of accepting and knowing who you are. When you are peaceful and loving, you then desire the very highest, you aspire to that which is beyond.

Violet:

> *I enter the inner-most part of my being. I am now there. I am centered.*

The whole purpose of life is to know who you are, that you are of God, and to return to that knowledge. And you do it by following the seven steps of the rainbow. You do this by releasing your body, releasing your emotions, and releasing your mind; entering a peaceful state, loving of others, desiring oneness with God. This is a natural sequence; you become centered.

In the last stage of being centered you say to yourself:

> *I am now one with my inner-self, a state which encompasses all of time, so that I just become aware of the totality of the now. I am only conscious of the present. I feel and sense this one moment in time …*
> *I just realize myself right now.*

We live in a three dimensional world that tells us there is yesterday, today and tomorrow. But when we are centered, we enter the spiritual realm and the only time is now. Reality is that there is no yesterday and there is no tomorrow. There is only the now.

At the conclusion of your centering experience you may exit the fourth state of consciousness by ascending up through the spiritual energy levels from violet to red — traveling in reverse — going through the rainbow in the return sequence: Violet, purple, blue, green, yellow, orange and finally red. You move from the inner oneness to the outer physical state.

How long will centering take to work?

According to Alexander and other spiritual masters, experiments show that it takes about twenty-one days to create a habit. Mark your calendar for twenty-one days and make sure — if need be enforce it on yourself — to center every day. After the three weeks, you really do not have to think about doing it anymore; it will have become automatic.

You are probably thinking: "All right, I do it for twenty-one days, it becomes automatic, I've created a habit. How long do I have to do it before I really see results in my life?"

The answer, according to Alexander, varies with the individual: "It cannot be said that within three months or six months or nine months you will see incredible changes. It is like exercising: The first week is the hardest, then it gets easier and easier. But you don't really see changes in your body for several months. Some people see results almost immediately; others take almost a year.

Suppose you don't center yourself every day? Suppose you forget?

Alexander said, "I'd like for you to think about how you drive your car. You have a steering wheel, and if you take your hands off of it, you may end up in a ditch. So you constantly have to make corrections. If you go off a little, just come back. The same applies when you're centering. If you get off course and take your hands off the wheel, so to speak, and quit doing it, what you've got to do is to take hold of the steering wheel again and direct yourself where you want to go — and that is to center on a daily basis."

Evaluating the Centering Experience

What happens during the "now" of the centering experience? Will you see visions? What comes to people who have led their minds into a restful, open receptive state?

Dozens of people we have talked with describe their ascent through a long tunnel which leads them toward a dim light that often becomes brighter. It is a peaceful voyage up the tunnel toward the promising brightness. Some people have told us they have gone beyond the tunnel into an area where they have dimly perceived saintly, gentle figures who welcome the seeker with beckoning arms. The tunnel with the dim light at the end seems to be a more common experience during centering. Others experience no sense of traveling or ascending; they describe a feeling of being totally connected to everything in their world — a oneness with all life and all things which the creator has provided. But whatever the nature of the vision, indisputably people return from centering refreshed, shed of worries, clean of unworthy thoughts, relieved of the clamors of the day, feeling more as an integrated part of everything that is.

The more you practice centering, the more effective you will become as a human and the more you will appreciate the growing awareness in your self that you are a marvelous, unfolding mystery within The Great Mystery, and that you have the power to make anything of your life that you wish.

Of course, there have been reports of remarkable centering experiences which are more specific in content and which reflect the higher degrees of consciousness that can be reached through unusual circumstances. Such a one was described by Charles Lindbergh in his book, *The Spirit of St. Louis*. It happened to him during his epic flight to Paris. All the conditions for centering were present as he sat alone in his plane almost adrift from his body:

"While I'm staring at the instruments, during an unearthly age of time, both conscious and asleep, the fuselage behind becomes filled with ghostly presences — vaguely outlined forms, transparent, moving, riding weightless with me in the plane. I feel no surprise at their coming. There is no suddenness to their appearance. Without turning my head, I see them as clearly as though in my normal field of vision. There's no limit to my sight — my skull is one great eye, seeing everywhere at once....

"All sense of substance leaves. There's no longer weight to my body, no longer hardness to the stick. The feeling of flesh is gone. I become independent of physical laws — of food, of shelter, of life. I'm almost one with these vapor-like forms behind me, less tangible than air, universal as ether. I'm still attached to life; they, not at all; but at any moment some thin band may snap and there will be no difference between us....

"I'm on the borderline of life and a greater realm beyond, as though caught in the field of gravitation between two planets, acted on by forces I can't control, forces too weak to be measured by any means at my command, yet representing powers incomparably stronger than I've ever known....

"Death no longer seems the final end it used to be, but rather the entrance to a new and free existence which includes all space, all time.

"Am I now more man or spirit? Will I fly my airplane on to Europe and live in flesh as I have before, feeling hunger, pain, and cold, or am I about to join these ghostly forms, become a consciousness in space, all-seeing, all-knowing, unhampered by the materialistic fetters of the world?"

From his moving experience, Lindbergh, like other men and women who have glimpsed "beyond the veil," was changed forever. He became a subtly different person. The feeling of power — of your own magnified self — to be realized from the discipline required to center daily, to go deep into the self, to explore the regions of the spirit, was captured by fencing champion Peter Westbrook, who briefly described what he called "the blazing moment," a moment when he was centered with his saber flashing during a sporting contest.

"At the peak of terrific effort when victory is at hand, when the blood is pounding in your head, suddenly everything becomes quiet inside you. Everything is clearer than ever before, as if somebody turned on a big spotlight. At this moment, you just know that you have all the power and sureness in the world and it's concentrated in your magic, in your whole body, and you are capable of doing anything. It's power beyond belief. And this is the moment, the blazing moment, you want to remember and hold on to for the rest of your life. It's a feeling you will work very hard for years to repeat."

Centering, as we have said before, is basically a form of meditation of which there are many expressions, as mountaineer Frank Smythe demonstrated in this statement from his book, *Mountain Vision:* "Physically you may feel but a cosmic speck of chemicalised dust, but spiritually you will feel great. For is not your vision capable in one glance of piercing the abysses of space? Is not your hearing attuned to an immortal harmony?..."

But without practice, as Alexander Everett pointed out, many people report difficulty recapturing high feelings, dramatic visions, that may occur during centering. Often, they don't have a workable philosophy or the basic under-standing to support spiritual experiences on which to base a better life.

Alexander observed that without understanding the Seven Laws of Life, the person who centers himself is missing the guiding principle, which make centering more purposeful and fulfilling. Following are the seven laws based on an explanation by the spiritual leader of Inward Bound:

"There are different types of laws with which we maintain order in our world. Man-made laws such as traffic regulations keep our society orderly. If a policemen observes you speeding on a highway, he will probably give you a ticket. Scientific principles such as gravity keep our planet orderly. If you release an object in mid-air it will fall to the ground. This is a demonstration of the law of gravity. There is another set of laws, natural laws, which when observed, provide health, wealth, happiness, loving rela-tionships and right occupations. If you are not in synch with these principles, then the natural laws are probably not being observed."

It behooves us all to understand the Seven Laws of Life because each one of us requires moral, ethical and spiritual guidelines by which we may aspire to a greater personal perfection. Do not be surprised if you are not familiar with the natural laws of life. In our hurly-burly world much of the emphasis on the philosophical aspects of life — studies that used to be part of the liberal education of a person — has been downplayed. Many people, without a reference guide of moral values, have become reckless, ignorant of who they are, careening through life like a rudderless boat in a confused sea. The Seven Laws of Life act as a directional finder, a compass that always points to "True North."

The Seven Laws of Life

Here are the Seven Laws, based on Alexander's words. Law number one is based on the concept that we are all one. The four kingdoms of life — human, animal, vegetable and mineral — all are created by the same God-source and are of that God-energy. Humanity is the only element that does not understand this oneness. As such, it is the only element that is out of synch.

The symbol of oneness is the circle. When two people get married, the ring, a circle, symbolizes that they have become one.

The second law comes straight out of the first. This is because the energy of man and woman as one is dual by nature. In the East, it is called the Yin and Yang, and this is the symbol of law number two.

Law number two embraces the two aspects of our being: the outgoing part which is the masculine, the doing part; and the incoming part which is the feminine part, the intuition. The female part is the wise one because it is the part that knows. Woman are intuitive, inspirational. The masculine represents love; males are the lovers and love is the highest energy that can be given. Once we know that both masculine and feminine natures exist in us, whether we are male or female, we can work to develop both of our natures to create a balance.

Put another way, Alexander explains, life is a female beingness, the mother, and love is the male, the outgoing doingness, the father. And the balance we are aiming for is that of moving love through our lives. It is symbolized in all of the great religions. In the Judaic teachings it is symbolized by the two pillars outside Solomon's temple. In the Catholic church, it is symbolized by the two large candles on the altar representing the male love and the female wisdom balanced.

Number three — The law of creativity.

The third law comes from the second law: When you take love and move it through life you get the result of light. For instance, when a man and woman have intercourse, they create a child. Another way to look at this is to consider that the interaction of male love with female intuition results in ideas. When you are doing what you love, when you love your work, the light of happiness will be the manifestation. We are on earth to give our intuitive talent to the world. This is manifested by the painter who creates pictures or the baker who creates bread. The question is what are we going to create? What light are we going to give to the world?

You may say, "I don't have a natural talent. I'm not a genius. Therefore, I don't have anything to give to the world." But the dictionary defines the word "genius" as natural ability. Everyone has a natural ability; you have only to claim your genius power to fill your highest good. And, of course, there are ways for you to discover your genius. Centering is one of them.

The symbol for law number three is the equilateral triangle, representing that the father-mother-child or love-life-light components are equally important. The third cannot exist without the other two.

The fourth law is the law of the fourfold nature of man.

There are four parts to man's consciousness. The first is the physical, which is the lowest. Then, there is the emotional, which is higher and controls the physical. The mental controls the emotional. The fourth and highest state of consciousness is the spiritual, which controls the mind. You may remember this definition of the consciousness of man from an earlier chapter. This explanation simply offers the definition in a little different light. The first three natures of man's consciousness are dual; physically you can hit or hug your neighbor; emotionally you can love or hate; mentally you can think positively or negatively. If you have good thoughts, you will have good feelings and good actions. This is expressed in the old Biblical quote, "As a man thinketh, a man is." But many of us have bad thoughts which we manifest in bad feelings and actions.

The good news is that we can control our thoughts by entering the fourth, spiritual state. This is the most powerful. For it controls the mind which controls the emotions, which control the body. It is our God-power which is not dual by nature, but just is. When we are in touch with spiritual perfection, we will think right, feel right and act right. This is what centering is all about: obtaining this fourth state of consciousness and bringing our four natures — spiritual, mental, emotional and physical — into balance.

As Alexander explains, "I want people to understand that they have this power. And when they realize it, their whole life changes from that moment forward. It did for me. I've never been the same since. That is because I realize I can do anything I wish, anytime I wish, because I accept that this spiritual, perfect God-power is within me. And every person can do likewise!"

The symbol of the balance — the fourfold nature of man — is the weathervane pointing to the cardinal points of the compass. The physical is in the west, the spiritual is in the east, the mental is in the north and the emotional is in the south.

Number five — the law of the five senses of man.

The five senses of man: Sight, hearing, smell, taste and touch, are gateways and operate through the four natures of man, which are the physical, emotional, mental and spiritual. For example, take the sense of hearing and apply it to Alexander when he conducts a workshop. Everyone hears Alexander physically because he has a powerful voice. It is very hard to sleep during his lectures. Some hear him emotionally because he gets excited and waves his arms about and that excites them too. Some hear him mentally and take notes for future reference. And some will hear him spiritually, for when he says something, they might say to themselves, "Oh, yes! That's right." They wake up to what they already know though they have never heard it before. That is because they already comprehended deep within themselves and that is knowing it spiritually.

Number six — the law of work.

One of the major principles of the laws of life is that you have to work. Unfortunately, we are brought up to believe that work is something we do Monday through Friday so that we can have pleasure on the weekend.

Actually work and pleasure should be identical. When you love your daily occupation your work becomes your pleasure. The people who are really creative and productive do not stop at the end of the day. They never wait to start again on Monday morning. They are doing all the time what they love because they love it. People who enjoy their work are happy, productive, and they make money. Until we find the work in life that we wish to do, the genius that is our gift will not be happy.

How do we find this natural talent? One way is to ask two questions of yourself: 1) What did I dream about doing when I was twelve years old? 2) What am I led to do intuitively? To receive the answer, touch the God-power within you by centering. You can also discover your natural ability by analyzing your personality traits as they relate to the colors of the rainbow. You read about the colors in the previous section on centering.

Number seven — the law of completion.

The seventh and last law really is not a law at all. It represents a summary of the six previous laws. It is the capstone of completion turning back to number one. That is why seven is considered the sacred spiritual number.

We start with one, the God-energy; we realize it is dual (two) in nature, which is the masculine and feminine. We realize when we combine these that we go to three and become creative. Also we realize we have four bodies to express that creativity. We have five channels through which to learn and grow. Six, we manifest. Seven, we are complete and whole.

It is the remarkable physicist Erwin Schrödinger, one of the towering figures in twentieth-century science, a man who ranked with Albert Einstein, who gives us a definition of the immortality of the human spirit — that essence with which we aspire to link in the act of centering:

"A hundred years ago, perhaps, another man sat on this spot; like you, he gazed with awe and yearning in his heart at the dying light on the glaciers. Like you, he was begotten of man and born of woman. He felt pain and brief joy as you do. Was he someone else? Was it not you yourself? What is this Self of yours?

"… What clearly intelligible scientific meaning can this 'someone else' really have? … Looking and thinking in [this] manner you may suddenly come to see, in a flash,… it is not possible that this unity of knowledge, feeling, and choice which you call your own should have sprung into being from nothingness at a given moment not so long ago; rather this knowledge, feeling, and choice are essentially eternal and unchangeable and numerically one in all men, nay in all sensitive beings. But not in this sense — that you are a part, a piece, of an eternal infinite being, an aspect or modification of it…. No, but inconceivable as it seems to ordinary reason, you — and all other conscious beings as such — are all in all. Hence this life of yours which you are living is not merely a piece of the entire existence, but is, in a certain sense, the whole; only this whole is not so constituted that it can be surveyed in one single glance…. Thus you can throw yourself flat on the ground, stretched out upon Mother Earth, with the certain conviction that you are one with her and she with you. You are as firmly established, as invulnerable, as she — indeed, a thousand times firmer and more invulnerable. As surely as she will engulf you tomorrow, so surely will she bring you forth anew to new striving and suffering. And not merely 'some day:' now, today, every day she is bringing you forth, not once, but thousands upon thousands of times, just as every day she engulfs you a thousand times over. For eternally and always there is only now, one and the same now; the present is the only thing that has no end."

Schrödinger makes clearer the value of understanding the Seven Laws, and if you reinforce them through centering and you apply them with sincerity, your whole life will change for the better. And you will understand the grand simplicity and the marvelous complexity of who you are which was so thoughtfully expressed by William Wordsworth in his *Intimations of Immortality:*

> Our birth is but a sleep and a forgetting:
> The soul that rises with us, our life's star,
> Hath had elsewhere its setting,
> And cometh from afar:
> Not in entire forgetfulness,
> And not in utter nakedness,
> But trailing clouds of glory do we come
>   from God, who is our home:
> Heaven lies about us in our infancy!"

11

Soaring Lessons for Runners

Here in this chapter you will discover some grand ideas for improving how you run, how you think about running and how running exercises can be a metaphor for how you can add to the spiritual depths of your life in ways you may never have thought of before.

"Running is just a physical activity, you've got to grind out the miles." So goes the familiar statement spoken by dozens of coaches and runners. Another old saw goes like this: "Running is a mind game, it's all in your head."

A different interpretation of running is advocated by people like George Sheehan and Joan Ullyot who insist that "Running is good for the soul and can put you in touch with the deep essence of life." Which approach to running do you favor, the physical, the mental or the spiritual?

Well, of course, you don't have to choose. It is possible to design a running program that supports all three of these human qualities. Indeed, whatever your purpose for running — competition, health, enjoyment, self-discovery — you will most assuredly advance that purpose if you view running as a total mind, body, spirit experience.

The training sessions recommended here are distilled from interviews with thirty extraordinary champions profiled in this book. All of them are Olympic gold medalists, world champions or trendsetters in their sports. Collectively, these champions who have excelled in running, archery, wrestling, shooting, Indy car racing, kayaking, mountain climbing, cross-country skiing, swimming and other sports have, without exception, said that what a runner thinks while he is running may have a greater impact on his performance than the distance, speed and frequency of his workouts. You will encounter this statement or a variation of it several times in the next few pages because the manner in which an athlete focuses on his sport may certainly help him reach into a deeper center of himself to develop a more effective level of personal functioning.

By now most of the readers of this book will have accepted the idea that there are indeed strong similarities between the athlete's concentrated mental focus on training for his sport and the frame of mind a worshipper at church, a devotee of yoga, or a practitioner of martial arts bring about when he seeks to enrich himself through consciousness expansion. We know that consciousness expansion can be achieved by several methods including hypnosis, prayer, meditation, biofeedback, centering and Zen sitting.

Given the similarities between sports and methods of expanding spiritual awareness, the question we seek to answer in this chapter is can sports people deliberately promote mind/body/spirit integration to improve performance? Can the kinds of experiences athletes have demonstrated in this book be systematically developed?

Of course, part of the answer to this question is clear. Yoga, meditation, centering, hypnosis and other methods of fusing mind/body/spirit are already being used by athletes and coaches in many countries, but generally there is still only slight emphasis in Western sports on evoking extraordinary displays of energy by such deliberate methods as meditation.

In his book, *The Joy of Running,* psychiatrist Thaddeus Kostrubala explained how athletic activity such as running in conjunction with meditation can generate the state of deepened awareness that can produce remarkable increases in energy:

"I liken ... running itself to one of the major techniques of meditation, and sometimes prayer, employed by virtually all disciplines both East and West: the constant repetition of a particular word or series of words, whether it be, 'Om, na pad na, om na,' or the Hail Mary. It matters little what value that particular philosophy or religion attaches to the use of the word, phrase or prayer. It is clearly intended to be an opening into another aspect of awareness. In short, by means of the repetition, the phenomenon sought — namely, the touching of another state of consciousness — is achieved. I think the same process occurs in the repetitive rhythm of slow long-distance running. Eventually, at somewhere between thirty and forty minutes, the conscious mind gets exhausted and other areas of consciousness are activated."

The energy that Kostrubala refers to has been described in various ways but the explanation for its source that we like the best was described by the author who wrote the Foreword to *Spirit of Champions.* He is Brian Luke Seaward with whom we talked about running as a state of meditation. Seaward said, "It is the present moment that we strive to capture with a meditating mind. For it is in the present moment that the universal mind resides — the omnipotent mind we seek reunion with.

"The universal mind only knows the present moment, for it has no concept of time. Unlike the human mind — which races from the past to the future with little time spent in the present — in divine consciousness there is only now. As hard as it may be to understand, the rules of space and time as we know them do not apply to nonlocal consciousness. In other words, the clock of the Master of the Universe is not calibrated to the human mind."

Seaward and others have observed that many athletes find running to be an activity that can lead the individual into a contemplative mindset which opens the way to the "present moment" of the divine consciousness, the unending state of "now."

Of course, it is when the individual, through the process of indwelling, comes into contact with his deeper self that he experiences a marvelous sense of release, a joyous freedom he has never known before.

As we've already discussed in this book, meditation practice need not be limited to a quiet retreat. Many runners have crossed the threshold, propelling themselves into a trance-like state often described as "the zone." It is when the individual comes into the zone that he experiences the deepest sense of gratification, when the power of the zone, as expressed through the individual, transforms him with an energy that is uplifting and limitless. Many athletes have credited the energy they found in the zone to astonishing performances, winning performances. Remember what happened to Bob Richards, the Olympic champion with an injured leg muscle who called on God to help boost him over the world record pole vault height to win a gold medal?

There are many ways to meditate. Running is one of them. But, whether you run, paddle a kayak, climb mountains or seek reunion with the source in the quiet of your bedroom, meditation should be practiced at regular intervals. By practicing with persistence, you will discover that the calmness and insight that comes to you will deepen, become more pervasive, influencing your thoughts and actions in a strong, positive way, increasing your ability to be more effective in whatever you choose to do in life.

Following are some ideas and suggestions to improve your skill in running and perfecting your insight to achievement levels you may have thought were beyond you.

New Frontiers for Performance Running

The basic physiological principles of training have been known for years. By fine-tuning these principles, runners can squeeze a few more hard-earned seconds out of their bodies. Conversely, by unleashing the potential of the mind and by tapping into one's spiritual wellspring, vast improvements are possible.

The strictly physiological approach to achieving athletic excellence, which is the dominant training approach in the United States today, can take an athlete only so far, and that is not far enough for anyone aspiring to achieve his personal best. During the past twenty-five years coaches, athletes and physiologists have developed somewhat standardized, descriptive names for the six different types of running workouts. They are: 1. over-distance (longer and slower than your average session), 2. strength (all activities intended to build muscle strength), 3. speed (intervals and sprints), 4. race-pace or actual racing, 5. technique (learning refined motions), and 6. recovery or easy volume (non-stressing workouts).

Until very recently, the science of athletic training consisted of finding a superior mix of performing these six workouts. This approach is no longer adequate. Mixing "physical" workouts fails to engage and develop the full talents and latent abilities of the person.

To make sports participation — for the dedicated athlete or for the daily exercise runner — as fulfilling and life-benefitting as it truly can be, and to reach a heightened level of personal excellence, runners need to recognize that there are new training methods that go far beyond merely "whipping the body into shape." New programs rely on the idea that we are mind, body, spirit beings, and if we are to achieve champion status in any endeavor, running or mountain climbing, our mix of "exercises" must also include activities to develop and strengthen the integration of mind, body, spirit which can be achieved through the Physical Meditation Workout. As we've already observed, meditation is a mental emptying ... so that the beautiful, the useful, the meaningful, and the peaceful can refill our mental storage cabinets. Meditation prepares our mind's garden by clearing out mental weeds so that fruit-bearing thoughts have a place to grow.

Most athletes periodically experience a plateau — a stagnant performance level. Plateaus are often the result of stagnant thoughts which have become embedded in the psyche, and they need to be replaced. The meditation workout is a great way to do this, especially for endurance athletes.

The Physical Meditation Workout

Pick a safe place to work out that is free of distractions. Avoid traffic congested areas or rutted trails that require you to focus on the external environment. Begin running slowly without any thought about the required motions of the activity. Free your mind from the burdens and bothersome details of daily life. Allow gentle thoughts to pass through you, neither resisting them nor dwelling on them. If they are valuable they will come back to you after the training session. Continue training until you have reached the efficient state which indicates your body has warmed up to the exercise. You will be breathing deeply but not straining for air.

Let the repetitive rhythm of each stride and your breathing be the mantra that keeps your mind free to receive insightful messages about performing your sport and about yourself as a human striving to improve himself. Allow your body to move as it determines best. Don't consciously interfere with your auto-pilot. This pilot may intuitively know a course and method of success yet to be discovered by the conscious you.

Practice the meditation workout for twenty minutes, but, absorbed as you are, you won't be able to judge whether five minutes or forty have passed. Experience will tell you what duration is best for you. I think thirty minutes is ample, which means you can complete a meditation workout within the framework of another longer training session.

The purpose of the meditation workout is to encourage your inner athletic self to become the dominant voice. And since it speaks in hushed and subtle tones, it requires a quieted mind to hear its message.

Your training session can be performed in a group, but alone or with others, silence is essential. It is a rare and much developed training team that can work together and support each other in this type of training. Groups will be more common in the future as the concept of mind, body, spirit integration becomes more widespread.

The Physical Visualization Workout

Medical, psychological and physiological scientists have proven conclusively that the mind can alter the physiological function and form of the body. This fact gives great credence to the establishment of transformative and performance-enhancing workouts which are available to all athletes, to any person who is prepared, for that matter. No single type of workout is more valuable to the athlete than the physical visualization workout.

Your body will adapt to a physical stimulus faster if it is also reinforced with an accompanying mental one. It's not very productive to go to the weight room and crank away on the weights when your mind is discouraging you with negatives: "What's the use, I'll always have wimpy arms." If you doubt that the mind can produce a physiological change in the body, answer this: "Do you believe that some people can make themselves sick by worrying and focusing on being sick?" Nearly everyone does. The flip side is also true; the mind can produce a positive change — there is much evidence supporting this statement. Your subconscious mind makes a million calculations per second as a result of managing your bodily functions. Direct this power to the changes you want for yourself.

Before your workout, decide what physiological change you most desire in your body; it could be increased leg strength, a leaner body, greater oxygen transport capability, or improved flexibility. For example, a runner may decide that she wants stronger thigh muscles for uphill running. Before the workout, she visualizes the quadriceps muscles and sees them becoming stronger and stronger. During her run, particularly on every uphill, she concentrates on the muscles growing stronger as they are being stimulated by the exercise. The more frequent the visualization, the better. Concentrate fully on the desired change and charge your thoughts with strong belief that the response will follow. Remember the remarkable performance of Marilyn King, who "visualized" herself winning her Olympic trials, even though her injured back had prevented her from any physical training whatsoever? But she won!

At the completion of the workout, sit down for several minutes, perhaps while you stretch, and deeply imagine that the physiological change you sought is happening. Many athletes currently visualize the performance they want — such as gracefully and efficiently running a sub-six minute mile or hitting a perfect forehand in tennis — which is a powerful performance-improving tool. We are suggesting that you go the next step. Also visualize your body making the desired physiological changes it is capable of initiating internally.

The Centering Workout

Champions know that running complements the main purpose of their lives. Running is not only compatible with the main purpose, but actually helps manifest that purpose.

Think of the exuberance and motivation you can have for your sport when you realize how it takes you toward your most cherished outcomes in life.

Before starting the centering workout, list three or four very important outcomes which you desire to have happen. As you enjoy your training session, think of all the ways that participating in your sport can help you achieve those outcomes. The passionate drive of men and women to fulfill their dreams is the power behind the most inspiring stories we read about. When your sports participation is hitched to your life's dream, you'll have the strength —

mental, physical and spiritual — to scale mountains and swim oceans if that is what it takes. To refamiliarize yourself with the centering procedure, turn to Chapter Ten.

The Passion Workout

The champions we have interviewed possessed a huge passion for their athletic endeavors. Were they born with a passion to run, row, shoot or swim? That's doubtful. Many of these champions didn't even start their sport as young-sters. Was their passion instilled in them by their parents or coaches? Perhaps. Often it grows from an idea into a burning desire. The champions we've interviewed undertook special activities and controlled their inner language so as to let their fondness for a sport grow into a love and then a passion of the body, mind and spirit. You can do the same.

Begin your passion workout with the affirmation, "I love to run." Start your workout without any intention of timing your miles or measuring success. Just run. As you proceed, make a mental list of all the reasons you love your sport. What does your body like about it? Your mind? Does it make you feel free, exhilarated, powerful? Is it exciting, relaxing, peaceful? Does it build friendships and cama-raderie? Does it make you feel connected to the earth, yet a part of something bigger?

Let your emotions run away with you. Yell with enthusiasm. Tell your training partners that you love life. Think of all the great things you have going for you. Think about exciting events coming up. This workout may take only fifteen minutes, but it can keep you high on your sport for an entire week. Without passion, it is seldom that someone goes the extra mile it takes to be a champion in sports or in life.

The Spirit Workout

This is a very special workout, not necessarily the most important or athletically beneficial one that you can do. But when "you have a good one," the spirit workout is among the greatest blessings you can give to yourself. There are probably hundreds of ways for an athlete to set forth on a spirit workout; here are three suggestions.

Spirit Workout Number One. Travel to one of your favorite settings in nature. If you live in a city, drive beyond the sights, sounds and impact of the city. Before you start the workout, look at all the plant life around you and realize that you have a special relationship with that life. It provides the oxygen you breathe, an environment that enhances your peace of mind. The fascinating dynamic earth upon which you stand supports your life. It furnishes you, all of us, with material for our homes, fuel for heat, and an endless array of life-giving things.

The purpose of your spirit run is not only to honor these relationships, but to actually draw energy from them.

As you run through nature, get in touch with the energy of the earth's flora and fauna. Try to physically sense that there is a greater energy in which you are immersed. Look at the trees and imagine that they can pass energy to you. Because you recognize this energy and honor your relationship with it, it will align with your energy, and propel you forward. In this manner, you can make the "spiritual wind blow to your back." Practice it and you will feel it.

Spirit Workout Number Two. Are you among the vast majority of Americans who acknowledge that when a loved one dies you feel his presence in a manner never before experienced, as if he were with you and encouraging you?

During your spirit run take all your loved ones, presently living and physically gone, in memory with you. Know that their energy is flying down the trail with you. Thank them for being with you and sharing their energy. They want the best outcomes for you, and your reflections on them will create a transference of positive energy.

Spirit Workout Number Three. Write down three personal prayers of thanksgiving and repeat these throughout your workout. Sample prayers might be: "Thank you, God, for blessing me with such a great ability to run." "God, grant me the wisdom to use my athletic learnings to make the world a better place for all of us." "Thank you, Mother of Life, for the opportunity to share this day with you."

It doesn't matter what the source of the extra energy is that you experience during a spirit workout, or the "realness" of it. If you feel it, it is real for you and available for your use.

The mind, body, spirit approach to training may sound exceptional, but from conversations with champions of all sorts, we have learned that without the willingness and persistent curiosity to investigate the depths within you, you will certainly miss out on the growth of your spirit which can open wide horizons to your future.

12

The Power of One

In this final chapter the ultimate question of "What is the purpose of life?" focuses all that we have observed and discussed in the previous pages.

As witnesses to the inexpressibly powerful nature of the human spirit in the men and women we've interviewed, we have concluded that a definition of Purpose must always be intensely personal, and it must always be related to acknowledgment of God in the soul. To arrive at this acknowledgment, each person must develop a spiritual insight.

In the pursuit of this insight, we have learned, people require definitions. For, as we wrote in this chapter, "We need them more than solutions because the act of defining what we seek is like building stepping stones into the future."

These stepping stones are described here and are designed to be helpful to all of us in affirming and reaffirming who we are, "...and who we hope to be as

— 265 —

we move deeper into the spirit to define, if not the whole mysterious purpose in life, then ours individually — as singular expressions of the Power of One within the embracing framework of the entire universe."

In an earlier chapter we made the observation that "it is comfortable, certainly not unsettling or challenging, to accept life as it comes to us, becoming neither more nor less than we have to be in order to prosper and get by and to be content with our ordinary beliefs and prejudices. This familiar way of perceiving ourselves does not take the soul into account.

The viewpoint expressed above says to us that we are limited creatures whose minds are confined to our brawn and bodies and to the present moment. When all our moments run out, our bodies will die and we will disappear into the abyss of nothingness.

As we observed earlier, what a bleak and terrible destiny!

Most of us are impatient with a viewpoint that ends life without a purpose and makes folly out of dreams of the extension of mortality beyond the grave.

While we are still pondering the purpose of life, most of us have progressed far enough to have developed a deep certainty that we are truly children of God in the spirit. And we hope to make the acts of our lives precious to ourselves and to others as reflections of the giving nature of the spirit within us — the spirit of which we are the Outward Expression. And this spirit has no ending.

Also we are learning with awe and wonder how inexpressibly powerful is the spirit. In these pages, in the stories of athletes and others who have achieved remarkable performances, we have discovered how they have been changed by experiences that left them transfixed and transformed. About the effort to become transformed, it was the German mystic Meister Eckhart who observed: "I tell you that no one can experience this birth of God in the soul without a mighty effort. No one can attain this birth unless he can withdraw his mind entirely from things."

So, now we are closing in on the purpose of life, as we see it. It certainly does require the development of spiritual insight, but in order to arrive at this insight, this sense of spirit in everything, one must live the right kind of life. To make this right kind of life, all of us require definitions. We need them more than solutions because the act of defining what we seek is like building stepping stones into the future.

Here, then, in the balance of this chapter, are the stepping stones we have found to be helpful to us in affirming and reaffirming who we are, and who we hope to be as we move deeper into the spirit to define, if not the whole mysterious purpose in life, then ours individually — as singular expressions of the Power of One within the embracing framework of the entire universe. This restatement of the words in the preface to this chapter underscores how important we feel it is to acknowledge that we are powerful units, like individual rays of sunshine, part of, but independent of, the great shining wholeness of the universe.

Definition of Spirituality

Spirituality is a personal inquiry into the mysteries of life. The study of spirituality is not limited to, but primarily concerned with, the ultimate question: Is there a Divine Force which created the universe and everything in it? If so, what does this Divinity require from each of us? This was the troubling question that Lyle Nelson asked of himself in 1977, when he was in Korea and was astonished when in a conversation with three Korean businessmen, he could not answer the question they asked him: "Lyle, what is the most important thing in your life?" He was chagrined because, by their attitude, the men made it clear that without a definition of life purpose, a person could not operate effectively; he would be as hampered as a man with a serious handicap.

The answer to the larger question of, "Is there a Divine Force?" is that there is no reply that can give proof of the existence of a Spiritual Master. But if the individual lives his life as if there is a Spiritual Master whose way is joy and giving, he will gradually develop deep insight and the world will come to be seen as one aspect of the Reality of the Spiritual Master. Often this happens when people like athletes experience an epiphany, a sudden transformation. But conversion comes to others in less-dramatic ways. Marty Kaplan, a former speechwriter for Vice President Walter Mondale, and a man who had described himself as a "cultural Jew, an agnostic, a closet nihilist," wrote in a _Time_ magazine essay that he was probably the last person "you'd figure would go spiritual on you." Yet in a moving statement, he observed:

"What attracted me to meditation was its apparent religious neutrality. You don't have to believe in anything; all you have to do is do it. I had worried that reaping its benefits would require some faith I could only fake, but I was happy to learn that 90 percent of meditation was about showing up.

"The spirituality of it ambushed me. Unwittingly, I was engaging in a practice that has been at the heart of religious mysticism for millenniums. To separate twenty minutes from the day with silence and intention is to worship, whether you call it that or not. To be awakened to the miracle of existence — to experience Being not only in roses and sunsets but right now, as something not out there but in here — this is the road less traveled, the path of the pilgrim, the quest.

"The God I have found is common to Moses and Muhammad, to Buddha and Jesus. It is known to every mystic tradition. In mine, it is the Tetragrammaton, the Name so holy that those who know it dare not say it. It is what the Cabala calls Ayin, Nothingness, No-Thingness. It is Spirit, Being, the All.

"I used to think of psychic phenomena as New Age flim-flam. I used to think of reincarnation as a myth. I used to think the soul was a metaphor. Now I know there is a God — my God, in here, demanding not faith but experience, an inexhaustible wonder at the richness of this very moment. Now I know there is a consciousness that transcends science, a consciousness toward which our species is sputteringly evolving, a welcome development spurred ironically by our generational rendezvous with mortality."

The path to spiritualilty is varied, but once arrived at, spirituality can become your personal way of interpreting the world and your reason for being in it. But spirituality does not mean that you passively turn over your life to an external force, nor is it necessary that you adhere to some religious doctrine. We have made a list of the benefits of spirituality. It follows.

What Spirituality Adds to Our Lives

1. Greater personal power comes to people as a result of their self-understanding.

2. Spirituality adds greater personal efficiency that results from mental clarity, which comes from an uncluttered mind.

3. Greater personal energy comes from being in sync with the universal flow of energy.

4. Greater personal energy comes from knowing that an internal well of energy resides in you, and you can learn how to tap into it.

5. Greater peace of mind comes from following your chosen life-path instead of stumbling along the most convenient path.

6. New relationships with people who live and explore life to its fullest depths develop instead of superficial associations.

7. Spirituality helps us to concentrate our physical and mental energies on those tasks which have in-depth significance for us. Without spiritual awareness, it is easy to join the disillusioned who may do good work without knowing if their work is doing any good. Spirituality makes your life more meaningful.

8. Spirituality helps us understand and harmonize with the laws of the universe, and spiritual development gives us the courage and conviction to determine those values we choose to live by, thereby establishing firmly our character, which gives clarity and purpose to our lives.

Spirituality Provides a Purpose for Life

If you live in the spirit, almost inevitably you will come to understand that the purpose of the human species is to survive and flourish, and that to accomplish this we have to evolve into more capable and intensified humans. Ultimately, our survival as a species will depend upon our higher evolution.

This concept, then, gives purpose to each of us as individuals. "To become all you can be" is what the Great Intelligence of the universe asks of us. To fulfill your purpose as a developing human, you must require excellence from yourself. You have the Power of One multiplied by the cumulative power of the universe to accomplish this task.

So finally, the purpose of life, according to every major religion and school of philosophy, whether written in modern times or surviving as a component of the Ancient Perennial Question, is: To strive towards the most accomplished, conscious, capable, enlightened being that you can fashion of yourself. This is the only sure path all of us must take to rejoin the spiritual source from which we came.

Fitting Spirituality Into Your Life

Nurturing spirituality is like growing a plant — it does much of the work by itself. Just as you must embed a plant in fertile soil, you must embed yourself in fertile values. This is not time consuming, and if you have followed the pathway established by this book, you have already begun. Of course, you have to nourish your spiritual growth. To do this, we've made a list of suggestions for you to follow:

A Plan for Spiritual Growth

1. Spend time walking in nature and listening to both the harmony of the universe and the special messages that may enter your mind at the time. Walking causes deeper breathing, which triggers special relaxation responses associated with exercising (yoga benefits). Relaxing helps to purify your mind.

2. Read as much about soul-care as you do about health, diet and cooking.

3. Memorize favorite spiritual sayings and include fifteen or twenty short spiritual poems or famous quotations.

4. Whether you accept spirituality or are ambivalent about it, search for opportunities to discuss it. In many homes, spirituality is as much in the closet as sexuality.

5. The first step to prepare for a spiritual life is to take up the right attitude toward life. Stop being an escapist! Face life squarely and get down beneath the surface where the truths and realities of life are to be found.

6. Recognize your compassion and responsibility for all forms of life. Inner peace comes through working for the good of all. We are all cellular entities in the body of humanity — all of us, all over the world. Each one of us has a contribution to make and will learn by searching within to define what that contribution is. But no one can find inner peace except by working, not in a self-centered way, but for the whole human family.

7. Meditate or center yourself as a method of cleansing your mind and getting in touch with the spirit in you.
8. Write your own creed and live by it.
9. Perform values clarification exercises; you'll find examples in this book. You must know what is most important in your life, or you won't develop a strong belief system.

You become a champion when you practice a plan for spiritual growth. A champion has an abiding sense of what is right and a growing awareness of his appreciation of the universe. He knows his place in it as the Power of One magnified by his link with other spiritually evolving humans.

The beloved poet Emily Dickinson understood the heart of the champion and expressed it with profound and simple words:

"We never know how high we are
Till we are called to rise;
And then, if we are true to plan,
Our statures touch the skies."

To order additional copies of

Spirit of Champions
Book: $14.95   Shipping/Handling $3.50

Contact: **BookPartners, Inc.**
P.O. Box 922, Wilsonville, OR 97070
Fax: 503-682-8684
Phone 503-682-9821
Phone: 1-800-895-7323